*The Book Lover's
Guide to the
Internet*

The
BOOK LOVER'S
guide to the
INTERNET

EVAN MORRIS

Fawcett Columbine • New York

A Fawcett Columbine Book
Published by Ballantine Books

Copyright © 1996 by Evan Morris

All rights reserved under International and Pan-American Copyright
Conventions. Published in the United States by Ballantine Books, a
division of Random House, Inc., New York, and simultaneously in Canada
by Random House of Canada Limited, Toronto.

http://www.randomhouse.com

Library of Congress Catalog Card Number: 96-96293

ISBN: 0-449-91070-9

Cover design by David Stevenson
Cover photography courtesy of Tony Stone Images
Text design by Debbie Glassmen

Manufactured in the United States of America
First Edition: June 1996
10 9 8 7 6 5 4 3 2 1

For Kathy, with all my love.

Thanks to my wife Kathy, who first encouraged me to write this book and was rewarded by being stuck with editing and proofreading the manuscript; to my siblings, for their encouragement; to my agent, Nancy Yost of Lowenstein Associates, for her good judgment and persistence; to my editor at Random House, Phebe Kirkham, for her awesome ability to coax order out of chaos; to Danny Choriki and Dan Poor, for their invaluable technical assistance; to the staffs of Interport, Bway and The WELL, and to all my friends, for their humor and support.

Contents

Chapter 1

WHAT IS THE INTERNET, WHERE DID IT COME FROM, WHERE IS IT GOING, AND DO I GET TO KEEP MY BOOKS WHEN WE GET THERE?

This is a book about books, reading, and the Internet: how to find books, magazines, newspapers, bookstores, and libraries on the Internet; how to find resources on the Internet of special interest to readers and writers; how to communicate with other readers and book lovers using the Internet; and how to use the Internet to publish your own writing.

The idea of doing this book came to me, appropriately enough, in a bookstore. I had already been exploring the Net for a while and had been amazed by the breadth and depth of reading material available on-line. So I was looking, that evening, for some sort of directory to fill in the gaps in my on-line explorations—a book about books on the Internet. Scanning the bookstore shelves for such a book, I realized two things. First, it occurred to me that the Internet itself was like a large but poorly organized bookstore or library, with thousands of volumes to read but no "Information Desk" and very few labels on the shelves. My second realization (after a prolonged but fruitless search) was that the book I was looking for, that Information Desk for the great on-line library that is the Internet, did not yet exist. Then a little voice said, "So write it yourself," and so I did. (Incidentally, I promised to take the little voice on a vacation when I was finished, so if you haven't bought this book yet, please do so now. I have a plane to catch.)

Whether you're a newcomer to computers and the Internet or you're already on-line, this book is intended to serve as a sort of treasure map of the on-line world, charting a path to the remarkable literary riches to be found on the Internet. But before embarking on a treasure hunt, it's traditional to tell the story of how the treasure wound up where it is, and so we shall. Once upon a time, there was a little global computer network . . .

WHAT IS THE INTERNET, ANYWAY?

Today almost everyone has heard of the Internet. Indeed, it sometimes seems impossible to pick up a newspaper or watch the news without being bombarded by nearly constant references to "the Net" or "the Information Superhighway." Even confining one's reading to the entertainment section of the daily paper is no escape—nearly every movie and restaurant advertisement is festooned with e-mail addresses and the cryptic "http://"

hieroglyphics that signify a site on the World Wide Web. Nearly every magazine now encourages its readers to voice their opinions via Internet e-mail, and even the New York City Ballet has established its own toehold on the Web (**http://www.nycballet.com**). (See Chapter 7 for a complete explanation of addresses on the Internet.)

What makes this sudden onslaught of Net madness all the more remarkable is that the Internet seems to have appeared and captured the public imagination virtually overnight. As recently as 1990, only a relatively small number of people, mostly those working with computer networks or at universities and research institutions, had ever heard of the Internet. A now-famous *New Yorker* cartoon of 1993, showing two dogs at a computer terminal (one saying to the other, "On the Internet, no one knows you're a dog"), was probably one of the first mentions of the Internet in a popular venue, and it almost certainly went right over most readers' heads.

So what is this thing called the Internet that has swooped down out of the blue and gobbled up the public consciousness?

Defining precisely what the Internet is has never been easy, and it's getting harder every day. Perhaps the most important thing to understand is that the Internet is not a "thing" at all—it's more of a phenomenon than a physical entity. The Internet itself is actually a network of networks, separate computer networks all over the world that are connected to each other to form a sort of super- or meta-network. Some of these constituent networks are small; after all, any two or more computers hooked together can be called a network. In contrast, some of the networks connected to the Internet are huge—academic and corporate computer networks serving tens of thousands of users.

Because the Internet actually consists of thousands of smaller, sometimes private, networks, exact (or even approximate) statistics on the size of the Net are notoriously hard to come by. But as of early 1996, it is probable that somewhere between 20 million and 50 million people are connected in some fashion to the Internet. The Internet is, in a word, *huge*.

A VERY BRIEF HISTORY OF THE NET

One of the curious things about the Internet is that it was never designed to be huge—quite the opposite, in fact. Ironically, today's wide-open and immensely popular Internet is a relic of the secretive and fearful atmosphere of the Cold War. The precursor of today's Internet was the Arpanet, created by the Advanced Research Projects Agency (ARPA) and funded by the U.S. Department of Defense in the late 1960s. Arpanet was designed to be a defense-oriented nationwide computer network capable, among other things, of withstanding a nuclear attack. The feared nuclear attack, thankfully, never came, and as the network grew over the years, it was gradually demilitarized, becoming a largely academic enterprise tying together researchers and students at colleges, corporations, and research institutions around the world.

Some of the features designed to permit the original Arpanet to survive nuclear Armageddon actually contributed to its gradual transformation into an extraordinarily versatile peacetime network. The durability of the original ARPA network was ensured by building in "redundancy"—data traveling from one computer to another could take any one of many routes to its destination. If part of the network were to be destroyed by a nuclear attack, the network itself would automatically route data by an alternate path. This clever little feature, carried over to today's Internet, makes effectively censoring the Net a daunting task: the Internet interprets censorship as a form of damage (who says computers are dumb?) and simply routes around it.

Arpanet was also designed to break the data stream transmitted over the network into little "packets" of information, like dividing a long letter into hundreds of individual postcards, so that if one packet failed to arrive at its destination it could easily and quickly be sent again. This method of sending data, called Transmission Control Protocol/Internet Protocol (abbreviated TCP/IP), is the "language" spoken by every computer on the Internet today. This common language allows all sorts of computers—from PCs and Macintoshes to huge mainframes—to exchange data over the Internet. TCP/IP also makes it possible to transmit many streams of data over the same network simultaneously, a capability that comes in handy when there are millions of people on-line at the same time.

The Internet grew gradually over the 1970s and 1980s but remained largely an academically oriented, strictly noncommercial network until the early 1990s, when commercial Internet service providers made it possible for the general public to access the Net. The boom in home computer ownership in the late 1980s had already led to the enormous growth of "on-line services" such as CompuServe, Prodigy, and America Online, as well as thousands of local "computer bulletin boards," but these services remained completely separate from the Internet until about 1993. When the gates to the Internet finally opened to the general public, what had been a slow trickle of interest turned into a torrent of new Net users, then swelled into the tidal wave of public fascination with all things Internet we see today. And that, dear reader, is how your local dry-cleaning establishment ended up with an e-mail address and a Web page (if you think this is an exaggeration, pay a visit to Tuggeranong Carpet & Upholstery Dry Cleaning at **http://cibc. anutech.com.au/new/103/**).

BUT WHAT DOES ALL THIS HAVE TO DO WITH BOOKS AND READING?

Oddly enough, an aspect of the Internet that has been largely overlooked in all the media coverage is one that newcomers notice immediately: the Internet is almost entirely text. The Internet is words, millions and millions of words. The unique riches of the Net, what a visitor can find on the Net and nowhere else, are, for the most part, things to read. The Internet brings together an enormous amount of textual information on nearly every topic under the sun, much of it either too arcane or too ephemeral to be easily found off-line. The Net can en-

hance your enjoyment of nearly any field of human en-
deavor—from cosmology to cosmetology, from rock music to foreign policy—but only if you're willing to read
what the Net has to offer.

True, the cutting-edge technological wonders of the
Net (pictures, movies, sound, etc.) may grab the attention
of the mass media, but at their best they amount to little
more than pale (and oddly pointless) imitations of television and magazines. Visit one of the Web sites maintained
by the major movie studios, for instance, and you can
download a 90-second video file promoting the latest
blockbuster—but why bother? If that same promotion
appeared on television, chances are you'd change the
channel. Visitors to one of the virtual art museums on-
line (the Louvre is a popular destination) spend long minutes waiting for masterpieces to appear on their computer
screens, only to be rewarded with fuzzy, colorless parodies
of great art nowhere near the equal of the reproductions
found in the most inexpensive magazine or paperback
book. The same is true for the tinny sound effects and
primitive video currently available on the Net—television
already does all that, and does it better. And although the
interactive multimedia capabilities of the Net are bound
to improve dramatically in the near future, the question
for many of us will still be "Why bother?"

What makes the Net unique, what it does especially
well, is the presentation of written material. There is a
strong case to be made for the proposition that the
people with the most to gain from the Internet today are
readers—those of us whose leisure time is most often
spent with a book, magazine, or newspaper, rather than

in front of a television set or at the movies. For us, the Net offers what television, and even traditional books and magazines, cannot: a nearly limitless library of writings of every kind, most of which have never been published and all of which are now, miraculously, at our fingertips. For readers, the Internet is an enormous book, written by millions of writers all over the world.

The Internet itself, in fact, resembles a book more every day. The most revolutionary technological innovation to hit the Internet in the last decade, the World Wide Web, uses programs called "browsers" to present information to the viewer in the form of "pages" that look, lo and behold, just like the pages of a book or magazine.

BOOK LOVERS ON THE NET

For the book lover in particular, the Net offers a vast array of resources, many of which are only available on-line. The world of literature on the Net is much more than just "books on-line," although there are plenty of those. Project Gutenberg (**http://jg.cso.uiuc.edu/pg**), one of several "e-text" (electronic text) projects, has set itself the goal of putting 10,000 e-texts on-line by the year 2001. They may well meet their goal—there are already hundreds of classics in the public domain (not covered by copyright) free for the asking on the Internet. Along with the well-known favorites of your school years, you'll find some of the more obscure works of famous authors on-line, making the Net's vast e-text archives a valuable resource for both the researcher and the casual browser.

Some of the resources awaiting readers on the Net mirror those available off-line, although the worldwide reach of the Internet can make it far easier to use them. It's possible, for instance, to order almost any book from dozens of on-line bookstores, whether you're looking for a current bestseller or a long-out-of-print rarity. Better still, thanks to the Web, you can now easily browse, and order books from, the catalogs of bookstores all over the world. Most major publishers also have Web pages, where you can search and order from their catalogs and often even read sample chapters of current best-sellers.

The evolution of on-line editions of general-interest magazines provides an especially interesting glimpse into the future of print publishing and the Net. After a tentative start on-line via The Electronic News-stand (**http://www.enews.com/**), which allows visitors to sample an article or two from a variety of magazines, *The Atlantic Monthly* (**http://www2.theatlantic.com/Atlantic/**) has taken the plunge and put most of the content of each issue on the Web for free, even adding special "on-line-only" items for Net visitors. It is likely that many more magazines will make the jump to full Web editions in the near future, supported by revenue from advertisements on their virtual pages.

The Net also offers a wide range of genuinely new resources for readers to be found only on the Net— Web-based magazines and journals, on-line book discussion groups and mailing lists, Web pages devoted to literature and authors and discussions of their works, on-line literary and book reviews (many of which are listed in Chapter 7), and, behind it all, a remarkable community composed of fellow book lovers and readers.

Many of the Web pages devoted to books and reading are treasure troves of information (and obviously Herculean labors of love on the part of their creators). A page devoted to the works of Mark Twain, for example (**http://web.syr.edu/~fjzwick/twainwww.html**), offers biographical and bibliographical information, links to electronic texts of Twain's works, information about mailing lists devoted to Twain, and links to other Twain resources (journals, archives, etc.). In the communal spirit of the Net, almost every such page also includes links to other pages on the Web devoted to the same or similar topics, plus often dozens of links to more general literary resources. Some of the most valuable pages for book lovers on the Web, in fact, are the indexes of resources, meticulously cataloging hundreds of links by author and genre. The page created by Piet Wesselman in the Netherlands (*Book Lovers: Fine Books and Literature* at **http://www.xs4all.nl/~pwessel**), for example, is a simply extraordinary collection of well-organized links to literary treasures around the world, and it rewards the visitor with hours of fascinating browsing.

Elsewhere on the Net, the emergence of serious Web-based magazines with built-in discussion areas, such as *Salon* (**http://www.salon1999.com**) and *The Utne Reader's Cafe Utne* (**http://www.utne.com**), heralds the advent of Web content unavailable anywhere off-line. With these experiments, the Net has given readers something genuinely new: the ability to peruse a journal or newspaper on-line, then immediately participate in an informed discussion with other readers around the globe.

Literary journals and book reviews have also sprung up by the dozens on the Web over the last few years. Some of these are on-line versions of print publications, giving readers a chance to sample a variety of views not always available at the local newsstand. Others are entirely on-line; some produced by university English departments, many the work of small groups of dedicated individuals.

Similarly, the ability that the Web grants nearly everyone to publish his or her own writing in a highly visible venue has already produced highly creative personal Web sites showcasing poetry or prose, as well as intriguing experiments in collaborative fiction.

The dozens of literary discussion groups, e-mail mailing lists, and newsletters on the Net have brought the kind of in-depth discussions previously found only in literary salons or university seminars to a worldwide audience. Some of the Usenet discussion groups devoted to books and reading are probably visited on a regular basis by 50,000 or more people, and many of these groups have developed into on-line communities in their own right. It's not unusual for a single discussion topic in **rec.arts.books**, for example, to garner 35 to 40 contributions from interested readers in a single week, and discussions of a controversial topic can sometimes last for months. **Rec.arts.books** is also the place to find periodic postings of FAQ (Frequently Asked Questions) files on a wide variety of book-related topics, including genre lists (such as *The Arthurian Booklist*, for devotees of Camelot) and the encyclopedic lists of bookstores in cities around the world compiled by Evelyn Leeper, who also maintains the extensive FAQ for

rec.arts.books itself. Of course, **rec.arts.books** is only one of many Usenet newsgroups devoted to books—there are many other groups devoted to specific genres, such as science fiction, and to particular authors, from Anne Rice to Shakespeare (see Chapter 7 for a complete list of such groups). Each group brings together newcomers and long-time fans, casual browsers as well as serious scholars, in an atmosphere of lively and informed discussion.

That the Internet has proven a fertile medium for readers and book lovers is not really surprising, given its history as a largely academic network intended to facilitate communication between researchers and scholars. Years before the first "newbie" (new Internet user) from America Online dipped his toe in the waters of the Net, the Internet was being used every day to exchange scientific information, to communicate between libraries, to discuss literary theory and cultural trends, and to share research data between institutions thousands of miles apart. Consequently, there was already an enormous reservoir of often highly sophisticated literary resources on-line before the Internet "went public." Behind the glitz and silliness of the "multimedia extravaganza" view of the Net touted by the mass media, this "old Internet" is still chugging along, growing every day.

THE CULTURE OF THE NET

Not only did the Internet exist long before it was discovered by the average citizen, but the inhabitants of the Net had developed over the years a distinct, genuinely intellectual culture embodying many of the best (and, yes, a few of the worst) traits of its academic origins.

First among the virtues of the culture of the Net is a respect for the free dissemination of information and knowledge. Almost all Net users are passionate defenders of the principle of freedom of speech—so passionate that most of the great debates that have taken place on the Net have centered on attempts to muzzle speech on-line, either by other Net users or by governments. Even offenders against the peace and sanity of the Net as a whole—such as the obnoxious "net kooks" who blanket the discussion groups of the Net with their rantings on a variety of imaginary grievances—are granted, by and large, the right to do so.

The Internet community is also a fairly remarkable experiment in democracy in action. Because the Internet is arranged as a network of networks intersecting at a variety of points, there really is no "center" to the Net, and certainly no "Internet Central" running the show. The government gradually gave up its central role in the development of the Net in the late 1970s, and even the National Science Foundation, which had funded the development of the primary network "backbone" of the Internet, has now bowed out of the picture. The Internet today is a largely self-governing community. In place of regulations legally governing what can and cannot be done on the Net, there is "netiquette," a framework of unwritten common law generally agreed upon by Net users that keeps things running fairly smoothly.

A Few Principles of Netiquette

The basic principles of netiquette are simply Internet-specific elaborations of the Golden Rule:

• Don't do anything to other Net users that you wouldn't like done to you.

• Don't publicly post e-mail another person has sent you unless the sender gives his or her permission.

• Don't send your messages to inappropriate discussion groups—especially if you're selling something and you post your pitch to all 14,000 groups on the Net (a practice known as "spamming"). Never type your messages IN ALL CAPS LIKE THIS—doing so is the Net equivalent of shouting, and it is enormously annoying to your readers.

• Don't engage in "flaming" or "flame wars" (exchanges of hate-filled e-mail or discussion group messages).

• Don't waste Net resources: for example, don't copy a file from a computer in Japan when the same file can be found closer to home, or don't simply quote what someone else has said in a discussion group and then just add "I agree" to the end of your message.

• In short, don't do anything that your fellow Net users might regard as annoying or destructive. The Internet, for all its global reach, is remarkably like a small town in many respects, and those millions of people out there are your neighbors. Be a good neighbor.

What's Mine Is Ours

Perhaps the most unusual facet of Internet culture, and the characteristic in which it departs most markedly from off-line culture, is the spirit of communalism that prevails on the Net. The governing ethic of the Net has always been that the resources of the Net should be free whenever possible and that one should not take from the Net without giving something in return. The Net itself was built largely by volunteers, and historically many people have viewed the Net (and some still do) as a grand experiment in Utopian Communalism. Without delving into the ultimate practicality of that vision, it is still possible to be struck by the amazing amount of hard work that has been freely given to the Internet community by its citizens. It's not just a question of "free stuff" on the Net (although there's plenty of that). Many of the best sites on the Net, especially those having to do with books and reading, show an extraordinary love of knowledge, an eagerness to share it, and a willingness to spend months and years contributing to the commonwealth of the Net.

Growing Pains

The Internet, of course, is just a mirror of society as a whole and becoming more so every day. Unfortunately, some of the less attractive aspects of both society and the Net have worsened of late, fueled at least in part by the opening of the Net to anyone who can afford or otherwise obtain a computer and a modem. What is called the "signal-to-noise ratio" (the proportion of content versus nonsense) sometimes seems to be dropping precipitously on the Net. The dominance in some areas of the Internet of a flamboyantly antisocial mentality, as well as a sudden influx of Net users who evidently view the Internet as just the latest incarnation of CB radio, has reduced some Net discussion groups to brutal and pointless shouting matches. The same yahoo factor has rendered Internet Relay Chat (the real-time chat facility on the Net) nearly unusable. And although pornography is not nearly as widespread on the Net as the mass media would have you believe, you'd never know it to judge by the number of "newbies" clogging some Net discussion groups with their requests for, as they put it, "nude pictures."

The World Wide Web, which has contributed enormously to the popularity and development of the Net itself, has highlighted another development on the Net in general and the Web in particular, which might best be called "the crisis of content." The sad fact is that much of what has been put up on the Web in the past two or three years is not worth the time it takes to access. The enormously democratic technology of the Web permits nearly anyone, anywhere, to put his or her thoughts and creations on the Net for the whole world to see. But this wonderful potential has led, sadly, to a global tidal wave of pointless, sophomoric, and downright boring "personal home pages" competing for attention with vacuous commercial Web sites promoting everything from Hollywood's latest blockbuster to rug shampoos and dog training emporiums. The prevalence on the Web of such cultural detritus has become intense enough to earn the Web an unflattering but sadly justifiable comparison to public-access TV ("Wayne's Web," or simply "the World Wide Waste of Time").

Whether the Net will survive this onslaught of mindless noise, as well as attempts by a variety of media

moguls to turn the Web into nothing more than an ad-
junct of television, remains to be seen. One can only
hope that it will, but, in the meantime, the trick to using
the Net without having the urge to shoot your computer
is to avoid the bad parts and seek out the good.

The good news is that there are true jewels amid the
rubbish on the Internet, and there are more of them
every day. The thousands of book lovers who engage in
serious and civil discussions in Usenet groups are a very
healthy sign. So, too, are the emerging cultural resources
on the Net devoted to women's issues and the concerns
of racial and national minorities. More generally, the increasing use of the Net and the Web to publicize cam-
paigns on behalf of human rights and to oppose censorship
around the world bodes well for the development of a
global network of mature, responsible citizens, and the
growing number of wonderful Internet sites created for
(and often by) children augur favorably for the future of
the Net.

There will always be a certain percentage of loud-
mouthed yahoos on the Internet. But the history of the
Net has also proven that there is plenty of room for the
rest of us to construct a literate, humane alternative community on-line.

BOOKS, THE NET, AND THE FUTURE OF READING

Given the perilous state of literacy in our culture, the
prospect of the Internet's becoming yet another vast
wasteland competing with television for the attention of a

nation of couch potatoes has deeply alarmed some commentators and educators. How can good old-fashioned books, they ask, compete with snazzy computer graphics? After we've all roamed the on-line world from our living rooms, who will be satisfied with a trip to the local library? Isn't the Internet really the final nail in the coffin of the written word? In many instances, these fears have been fed by the breathless predictions of chirping cyber-evangelists who seem to think that a bookless future would be a good thing.

One can hardly blame the critics of the Internet for being alarmed by the portrait of the future cheerfully painted by some cyber-prophets, where libraries are supplanted by computer banks and the printed word exists only as an ephemeral image on a computer screen; where books themselves have been replaced by handheld computerized readers, and where even the need to frequent bookstores is obviated by the instantaneous delivery of "texts" over the omnipresent network; where electronic mail has superseded all other written communication, so that never again will we be burdened with trying to decipher a loved one's idiosyncratic handwriting; where true human memory has been replaced by data storage, and the cultural life of a nation can be loaded onto one giant hard drive; where society itself has fragmented into isolated individuals, numbly clicking their way from one "cool thing" to the next, bathed in the pale glow of a computer screen. One need not be a Luddite to find such a future appalling—as Samuel Goldwyn once said, "Include me out."

No one can promise that such a dire future will not

come to pass, and it is true that there are, even today, some disturbing signs of the damage computer mania can wreak on the world of books and reading. Among them is the destruction of "old-fashioned" card catalogs at many libraries in favor of dubious data systems that often make it more difficult to locate a particular title. Alarming, too, is the fashionable but utterly fraudulent practice of rating the educational competence of a school by the number of computers found in its classrooms.

But the dreadful vision of a bookless world is not likely to come true, at least in part because the technological wonders of the future are never quite as shiny and efficient (thank heavens) when they actually arrive as they were promised to be. Electronic books are unlikely to ever replace real books, simply because real books are, and will continue to be, *better*. Books don't need batteries; books don't wear out; you can take books to the beach or into the bathtub (try that with a computer), and you can write an inscription in a book you love and then give it as a gift that has few equals in emotional significance. Human beings may not have meant to create something as wonderful and magical as books, and we certainly never dreamed at the time that we were inventing an "information storage and retrieval system" as versatile and adaptable as books, but we love our books and we're not about to give them up. The same goes for handwritten letters, and libraries with real books on the shelves, and bookstores where you can browse the shelves for a whole long afternoon. We have to be willing to fight to preserve these things because we know that they are, and will continue to be, important to human society.

The choice, ultimately, will be ours, because society is built by human beings, which brings us back to the Internet. The Internet is a computer network, largely accidental in origin, built in fits and starts from spare parts, *and that's all it is.* The Internet is not now, and never will be, a substitute for, or even "a quantum leap" in, reading and education. Anyone who tries to tell you differently is selling snake oil, and trying to pick the pockets of future generations to boot. No one, least of all children in school, "needs" the Internet, any more than they "need" computers in the first place.

The Internet is simply a communication tool by which we can expand the experience of reading and learning by bringing resources and people closer together. The enduring contribution of the Net to reading and literacy is likely to be the discussion groups, research resources, and on-line communities of readers and book lovers that will add to our appreciation of, not substitute for, real books and the knowledge gained from reading them.

Chapter 2

❖

HOOKING UP: SIMPLE WAYS TO CONNECT YOURSELF TO THE INTERNET

The first order of business for anyone interested in what the Net has to offer, of course, is to get connected to the Internet. Until just a few years ago, hooking up to the Net was a daunting proposition. Commercial access to the Net for individuals was virtually nonexistent, and even if you happened to have access through a university or similar facility, actually using the Internet usually required mastering the arcane syntax of the Unix operating system that serves as both the bedrock and lingua franca of the Net. Unix as a computer operating system has many advantages, but user friendliness is emphatically not among them, and clearing the Unix hurdle to get on the Net in the olden days (way back in 1990) often required making the acquaintance of someone known as a "Unix wizard" or "Unix guru." Wizards and gurus are not the hallmarks of a simple technology—after all, when's the last time you needed to go looking for a toaster guru?

But even in a world of increasing complexity, some things mysteriously get simpler, so brace yourself for some good news: over the last few years, hooking up to the Net has become a genuine no-brainer. It is now much less difficult than programming a VCR, and only slightly more challenging than using a microwave oven. In fact, if you've bought a computer recently, and it came with a built-in modem, "jacking into the Net" may be as easy as plugging your computer into the nearest telephone jack. But even if your computer is an ancient hand-me-down from your daughter the chemical engineer, the Net is well within your reach. Best of all, you need never learn a single Unix command.

How you'll be able to hook up to the Net depends on who you are, where you live, and what sort of computer you own. In most cases, you'll have a choice of access methods among which you can choose based on how much time you want to spend on-line (and how much money you wish to spend doing it). One of the best features of the Net, however, is the inherently democratic nature of the basic technology itself. We're all on the same Internet: the lucky fellow in a trendy Soho loft who cruises the Net using a $14,000 Silicon Graphics workstation hooked to a high-speed direct network link sees essentially the same *information* as the retired schoolteacher who uses an ancient 286 PC to dial into a freenet in rural Idaho. To squeeze the overworked Information Superhighway metaphor just a little, we'd all like to travel in a Rolls-Royce, but there isn't anyplace you can go in a Rolls that you can't get to just as well in a Ford, or even a Yugo. If you're operating on a tight budget, you might not see all the bright colors and fancy graphics that the Net-privileged do, but e-mail, discussion groups, and mailing lists will look exactly the same to you as they do to Bill Gates himself.

Equipment

You really need only four things to access the Internet: a computer of some sort, a communications software program, a modem (a contraction of "modulator/demodulator," a little electronic device that allows your computer to communicate with others of its ilk over a telephone line), and a telephone connection. Each of these four basic requirements can be satisfied in a range of ways, from the simple (and inexpensive) to the arcane (and ruinously expensive).

Computers

Almost any sort of computer can be used to hook into the Net. I say "almost" only because there are some computers so thoroughly obsolete (the Radio Shack TRS-80 springs to mind) that trying to find communications software to use on them wouldn't be practical. Any IBM-compatible, Apple Macintosh, or Amiga computer, however, is a definite candidate for Net use. The only limitations of older computers are that the software will have to be text-based (rather than a graphic interface such as Microsoft Windows) and that the access (modem) speed supported by your computer may be somewhat on the slow side. You won't see any pretty pictures if you're using a text-only communications program, but there's a silver lining to text interfaces: they're much faster than graphic programs—fast enough that, in many cases, a text-only computer operating on a "slow" modem link will often actually deliver information from the Net much more rapidly than a fancy Windows program via a high-speed modem. Many folks who have access to graphic applications actually choose to use text-only programs for precisely this reason.

On the other hand, if you're considering buying a new computer, there are a few general points to keep in mind that will make your on-line life easier:

• Get as much memory (RAM) as you can afford. Many entry-level computers come with 4 megabytes of RAM, but 8 megs is the minimum needed to run most World Wide Web browsers smoothly, and 16 megs would be a very wise investment.

• If you buy a computer with an internal modem, be sure to get one that is 28,800 baud (baud is the measure of modem speed, roughly equivalent to bits per second, or bps). Make sure that the modem actually transmits and receives data at that speed: some computers are sold with fax modems that send faxes at 14,400 or 28,800 baud, but that drop down to 9,600 baud for data (on-line) connections.

• Get the biggest hard drive and the largest monitor

screen that you can afford. A 17-inch monitor and at least a 1-gigabyte hard drive will repay your investment with freedom from eyestrain and anxiety. Peering at a small, dim screen while you worry about whether you have enough disk space to download that picture of the National Book Award Limbo-Dancing Finalists is no fun at all.

• Finally, some free consumer advice: Do not buy your computer at a store that also sells washing machines, aluminum siding, tube socks, or carpet remnants. Do not buy your computer at a store that sells only one brand of computer, or sells only brands that you've never heard of. And if the salesperson tells you that the monitor and keyboard cost extra, you're in the wrong store.

Buy a few computer magazines (*PC Magazine, Macworld,* and *MacUser* offer comprehensive comparisons of systems, for instance), browse through the ads, then either go to a reputable computer store or order your computer by mail from a major manufacturer. You'll be glad you did.

Software

To access the Net or on-line services, you'll need some sort of communications software, the program that controls your modem and presents the on-line world to you on your computer screen. There are a vast array of communications programs out there, and which one you use is governed largely by how you access the Net. If you buy a new computer, chances are good that it will come with the software for at least one on-line service already installed. If not, nearly every computer magazine these days comes in a plastic bag with a disk containing software from one of the on-line services. If all else fails, just call the service you're interested in and a representative will be thrilled to send you free software.

On the other hand, if you access the Net through an account at work or at a university, you either will be given or can easily obtain the requisite software from your system administrator. Community freenets (see page 31) usually leave it to their members to obtain their own software, but the folks who run your local system will be happy to point you in the right direction, usually toward a standard commercial communications program costing less than $100.

Independent local Internet service providers, another route to the Net, almost always supply free software with new accounts, although the "free" software is often "shareware," meaning that if you decide that you like it and keep using it (past about 30 days), you're bound by the shareware honor code to pay the developer a small fee (usually about $25).

Modems

As I mentioned earlier, a modem is the little gizmo that allows your computer to communicate with other computers over a phone line. If your computer didn't come with a built-in modem, you'll have to buy an external model that attaches via a cable to the communications port on the back of the computer. The phone line then plugs into the modem. Piece of cake.

Because the modem will be your link to the Internet, it's important to get the fastest model your computer can support. With a fast modem, images and text will snap up onto your screen, while a slow modem will give you plenty of time to make a pot of coffee while you wait. Even if you drink a lot of coffee, keep in mind that you'll probably be paying by the minute for the time you spend waiting, so buying a fast modem can save you money. (This is a good argument to use on a Net-ignorant mate who'd rather use the money for something silly, like shoes for the kiddies.)

Modems, like computers, have undergone a rapid evolution. In 1992 a 2,400-baud modem was considered reasonably zippy, but today 28,800 baud is the new standard. Fortunately, prices of fast modems have fallen substantially over the last few years, and a 28,800-baud modem (called a "twenty-eight-eight" by the Net cognoscenti) that ran $400 in 1993 can be had for less than $200 today. Resist the temptation to make do with a slower modem: the difference between a 14,400-baud modem and one running at 28,800 is more noticeable than you might think. A few on-line services still offer 14,400 as their highest access speed but eventually they'll all switch to 28,800 (and in the meantime, your 28,800 modem will work perfectly well at the slower speed).

If you own an older computer, it's important to check whether it can support one of the new fast modems. Because of the configuration of their communications ports, some older machines may be unable to support speeds of more than 9,600 or 14,400 baud, so check your user's manual. If this is the case with your computer, the best approach is to buy the fastest modem your machine will support (with the consolation being that you'll be getting a bargain price on a new, but slightly slow, modem). If you end up accessing the Net in a text-only mode, you won't really be able to tell the difference in modem speed anyway.

As is the case when buying a computer, buying a modem from a reputable dealer is worth the effort required, and sticking to recognized brands is especially important. U.S. Robotics, Hayes, Supra, and Motorola modems are all good bets.

Telephone Lines

Obviously, accessing the Internet pretty much presumes that you have a telephone line to work with. Unless you're hooking up to the Net from an office or a university dorm room, you'll probably be using a modem to dial into a host computer of some sort that will be your gateway to the Internet.

About the only choice you have in terms of a phone line in most locales is how many to have. Keep in mind that anyone who tries to reach you while you're on-line will get a busy signal, so if you find yourself spending a few hours each evening on-line, you may want to look into getting a second line put in. Don't let the phone company tell you that you need a special data line for a modem—you don't. If later on you have problems with the line you use with your computer (especially excessive line noise, which can seriously degrade throughput, or data transfer speed), tell the phone company service reps that you use the line for a fax machine. They seem to understand fax/phone problems better than computer/phone glitches.

The lowly computer–telephone line hookup will be undergoing a major transformation over the next few years, one that will make any modem you own obsolete (go ahead—groan now and get it over with). The advent of home service high-speed digital, or ISDN (Integrated Services Digital Network), lines will double or triple current data transfer speeds. ISDN service is already available from phone companies in many areas, although the price of such connections is still rather high for all but the most dedicated Nethead. Still, we know that ISDN (or something like it) is on the way simply because modem manufacturers, like the dog that did not bark in the Sherlock Holmes story, have given up on developing standard modems faster than 28,800 baud.

Of course, if you eventually decide that you *really, really like the Net a whole lot* (more than buying food or paying the rent, for instance), you may choose to sign up for a high-speed T1 or T3 data connection directly into the Internet itself. At between $1,000 and $3,000 per month, not counting the requisite hardware, this is an option you may want to sleep on for a while (and then discuss with your spouse, who will almost certainly tell you to shut up and go back to sleep).

GATEWAYS TO THE INTERNET: HOW TO PICK A SERVICE PROVIDER

Once you have all the equipment you need to connect to the on-line world, the next step is to find something to connect to—a service provider. There are many different types of service providers, offering different levels of access to the Net.

Free (or Nearly Free) Access to the Net

Picking a service provider to hook you up to the Net used to be fairly simple: if you worked for a university, a research lab, a government agency, or a defense contractor, you were automatically wired into the Net, because these institutions thought it important that their employees and students be able to communicate via the Net. Of course, the only people to talk to on the Net were other folks who worked for universities, government agencies, etc., but even at this early stage many folks decided that the Net was very cool. The practice of university graduate students prolonging their connection to their alma mater simply to feed their Net habit was (and still is) not uncommon.

The majority of users probably still access the Internet via an account at one of these institutions. (Exact statistics on Net usage are notoriously hard to come by, but institutional access is especially prevalent outside the United States, Canada, and Europe, commercial on-line services being virtually unknown in most of the world.) In many cases, users of these systems also can connect from home by dialing into their work computers and jumping from there to the Net.

All this is relevant for two reasons. First, you may already be a winner: if you work at an institution or corporation that uses a local-area network (LAN) to tie its workstations or PCs together, ask your system administrator if you can access the Net from your desktop computer. Believe it or not, some employers actually think that giving their employees Net access is a good idea.

Second, if you're a graduate of a nearby university, you may be eligible for a dial-up account on your alma mater's system, which is almost certainly a gateway to the Net. Some especially savvy universities have begun to offer Internet accounts to alumni who pony up contributions to the annual fund-raising drive. Just call the alumni office and ask if yours is among them (don't flinch—after all, you don't have to give your name unless they say "yes").

If you do manage to swing this kind of account, it's likely that it will be text only, but, if nothing else, it's a good way to test the waters of the Net. If you decide that you like what you see but don't like the way it looks, you may be able to improve the interface by asking your system administrator if he or she will allow you to use a program called a "SLIP emulator." Such a program lets you use graphic software (provided your computer is agreeable), including such "killer apps" as the Netscape Web browser. If your sysadmin agrees to the idea, these programs (MicroMind, Inc.'s *SLIPknot* and Cyberspace Development Inc.'s *The Internet Adapter* are two popular types) are readily available on the Net itself.

If you don't happen to work for the Defense Department or the like, your boss won't let you explore the Net from your desk, and an account with a university is not an option, your next stop should be the local freenet, if your community is lucky enough to have one. Freenets, as the name implies, are free bare-bones Internet service providers, often subsidized by local governments and businesses. They're more common in the rural west and midwest, but the trend toward universal publicly available Net access is one whose time (we hope) has come. Your local library is probably the best place to ask about an available freenet—in fact, libraries in many cities and towns now have open-access Net terminals available for use on a walk-in basis at no charge. If you do hook up to a local freenet from home via phone, you'll be dealing with a basic text-only interface. But smile—it's free!

Many cities and large towns also have local bulletin board systems (BBSs). BBSs are small systems (often run out of the owner's home) that cater to discussions among members on a variety of topics and usually offer software libraries and games. Many BBSs are inexpensive or free to join, and some have limited connections to the Internet (typically only e-mail). *Computer Shopper* magazine carries listings of the thousands of small BBS systems in the United States.

Commercial Internet Services

If you're not eligible for any of the free or very low cost options discussed above, you'll have to bite the bullet and pay for access to the Internet. Sobering as this prospect may seem (who needs another expense?) it's just a matter of perspective—after all, a premium account with unlimited hours on a first-class service provider will still probably cost you less per month than cable TV.

Obtaining commercial Internet access is usually just a matter of choosing between two principal alternatives: the large national (and, in some cases, international) on-line services and an increasingly broad range of Internet service providers, or ISPs.

ON-LINE SERVICES

On-line services, such as America Online, CompuServe, and Prodigy have become so visible in popular culture that an introduction seems unnecessary. America Online (also known as AOL) in particular seems to have decided to take all our minds off the problem of global warming by threatening to bury us beneath a worldwide 10-foot-deep layer of its ubiquitous free software disks.

Surveys have shown that thanks to the on-line services' advertising barrage of the last few years, the average consumer is now hopelessly confused about the relationship between the on-line services and the Internet. Most people assume that the big on-line services *are* the Internet. But the on-line services and the Net are, emphatically, not the same thing. Until quite recently, in fact, the on-line services had, quite literally, no connection to the Internet at all. Each on-line service was a kingdom unto itself, and even sending e-mail from one service to another was often difficult or impossible. With the growth of the Net, on-line services gradually have opened up to the outside world of the Internet, thus giving their customers access to the wide variety of resources available on the Net.

While the Internet itself is a global network of networks with no center, each of the on-line services has a definite center: the huge mainframe computers that form its foundation. Each of the on-line services is a distinct network to which you connect your home computer over a telephone line. Only subscribers can access the features found on the on-line services, which are all timed—every minute you're on-line (with the exception of certain free customer service features) costs money.

Each on-line service, though you'd never know it from their advertisements, offers pretty much the same standard features: news, weather, and sports reports, on-line versions of popular magazines and newspapers, an on-line encyclopedia, forums or discussion areas devoted to a wide variety of topics, hobbies, and interests, and, of course, extensive computer sections with listings of software available for downloading. Most services also feature "chat rooms," or real-time discussion areas where subscribers can converse (by typing) with anyone else who happens to be on-line at that time.

Every service has a few unique features that set it apart from the others, or a slant that gives the service character. CompuServe, for instance, boasts extensive connections to computer and software manufacturers, so if you're looking for advice on a particular brand of digital widget, CIS (CompuServe Information Services) may be the place for you. Occasionally a service will put considerable muscle into trying to change its spots. Prodigy, for instance, which once sold itself as an especially good choice for families with children, is now striving to appeal to young singles by establishing adult-only chat rooms and running trendy ads evidently aimed at banishing its stodgy image.

All the major on-line services now boast some form of gateway to the Internet, although not all of them give

their customers access to all of the features of the
Net. These services also supply some sort of World Wide
Web browser program, e-mail, and some form of software to read Usenet newsgroups (Internet-wide discussion groups).

The pros and cons of subscribing to one of these
services are the topic of endless debate and beyond the
scope of this book, but several points in favor of using
them are worth noting, especially if you're a newcomer to
the on-line world:

• Each of these services has a great deal of native content, features that are not available on the Net as a
whole. Each offers a particular selection of newspapers
and magazines, and several devote substantial space
to book discussion groups, writers' forums, etc. Your
best bet is to check the publicity materials for each service or enroll in a trial account (see below), and if something one of them carries strikes you as incredibly neat
("Holy cow! Plumbing Frontiers On-line!"), go ahead
and subscribe.

• These services have prospered by making getting on-
line a painless, nonthreatening experience, even for the
most technically inexperienced user. If it's comforting to
know that technical help is just a phone call away any
day of the week, you may want to go this route.

• Recognizing that the Internet can sometimes be a
confusing place for newcomers, all of these services have
devoted a great deal of effort to making the jump from
the cozy security of their service into the Internet as easy
as possible. Help files and tips on everything from how

to behave on the Net to how to find a particular site are offered to every customer. Anyone who actually reads all the informational materials these services offer their users before they access the Net will know more about the Net than many people who have used the Internet for years.

• All of these services offer trial accounts, usually 10 or 15 free hours, in which to check out what the service has to offer. Getting a free trial account usually involves giving the service credit card information so that billing can begin as soon as your free time is used up, but such trial accounts can be a good way to choose a service that you really enjoy.

There are, on the other hand, some definite disadvantages to subscribing to one of the major on-line services:

• The large on-line services are relatively expensive—usually about $10 per month for anywhere from 5 to 10 "free" hours. (This is a rather remarkable departure from the usual meaning of the word "free"—if 5 hours costs $10, that's called $2 per hour where I come from.) Ten "free" hours per month may sound like a lot of time, but it really isn't: most people, especially when they're just starting out, go over the ten-hour limit. Once your "free" time is used up, things get a bit more expensive, usually $3 or $4 per hour. It's very easy to rack up charges of $50 or more in a single month without realizing it, and parents who plan to let the kiddies take full advantage of the educational features of these services would be well advised to apply for a second mortgage before enrolling in an on-line service. In contrast, many independent Internet service providers (see page 41) offer accounts for $20 per month, which include an unlimited amount of on-line time. A user who pays an Internet service provider $20 per month for unlimited time, but who actually spends 40 hours on-line in a given month, would be paying America Online, for example, $113.20 (based on AOL's rates as of early 1996) for the same amount of access. Just the fact that on an Internet service provider you aren't watching the clock and worrying about spending too much money can make the whole on-line experience much more pleasant.

• Customers of an on-line service usually are locked into using that particular service's proprietary software, which is rarely equal to the best Internet access software available. Some of the software is so poorly designed as to constitute a real barrier for users trying to access the Net. Stung by criticisms of their software, both CompuServe and America Online have reconfigured their systems to allow customers to use superior third-party software, such as the Netscape World Wide Web browser. Of course, such arrangements still require paying the on-line service's hefty hourly connection charges.

• Some of the on-line services censor what their customers can access on the Internet. To mix a few metaphors, if Big Brotherism gets your goat, the paternalism of the big on-line services may not be your cup of tea. Ironically, their zeal to censor what adults can see does not necessarily make these services a good choice for parents concerned about their children's safety on-line (see Note to Parents, page 39).

• Because access to the Internet is routed through

centralized mainframe computers and overburdened networks, customers often discover that using an on-line service is an infuriatingly slow method of surfing the Net. For example, Web pages that load in Netscape on a 14,400-baud SLIP/PPP connection in less than 30 seconds can take up to five minutes to load in the America Online browser on a supposedly equally fast connection. Such delays will give you plenty of time to consider that you are paying in the neighborhood of five cents per minute for the privilege of twiddling your thumbs.

• Speaking of money, keep in mind that if you live in an area without a local access number for the service, you may have to pay a surcharge to use the service's special "800" access lines, sometimes as much as $6 per hour or more on top of the basic hourly charge.

Having said all this, I must note that a major on-line service is probably a good way to check out the Net and decide whether to proceed to a more evolved connection. If you decide that you really like browsing the offerings of one particular service for just a few hours every month, fine. Millions of people are happy doing just that. However, if you decide after a few months that the lure of the wide-open Net is too strong to resist, a flat-fee independent Internet access provider is probably in your future.

In terms of a specific recommendation among the various on-line services, I would vote for Prodigy. Its Web browser is outstanding, and its "Books" and "Writers" resource areas are truly exceptional, worth the cost of a subscription in themselves.

My only firm "thumbs down" vote goes to America Online, based on the relentless vapidity of the service as a whole, its seriously flawed software, and the considerations outlined in the accompanying Note to Parents.

Because the major on-line services change their pricing structure fairly frequently, it's best to contact each service for information on current rates. Software for each service may be obtained via the same toll-free number.

America Online: 800-827-6364
CompuServe: 800-848-8199
Microsoft Network: 800-386-5550
Prodigy: 800-PRODIGY

Note to Parents

There has been much discussion in the popular media, and several genuinely alarming news reports, about the availability of pornography on the Internet, as well as the threat posed to children on-line by pedophiles. While in many cases the extent of these problems has been exaggerated, the concern felt by parents for their children's safety while on-line is entirely justified. A few points on this subject:

• The availability of pornography on-line has been overstated. While it does exist, it takes a concerted effort to find it, and the trend on the Net has been to make pornography more difficult, not easier, to access. Ironically, this is due to the desire of commercial pornographers to make money. Most sites on the World Wide Web containing pornography, for instance, now charge an access fee via a credit card, effectively barring most children.

• Most of the truly obnoxious visual material on the Internet is posted as multipart binary files in certain Usenet newsgroups. ("Obnoxious" here includes more than just sexually explicit images. Murder scenes and autopsy photographs are commonly posted in some newsgroups.) Fortunately, from a parent's point of view, the steps involved in merging, decoding, and viewing these files on a home computer are fairly technically complex; thus it is impossible for anyone to "stumble across" the material contained in these files. Unfortunately, several of the larger on-line services have seen fit to include the capability to easily and automatically decode and view these files in their latest software, thus making the process quite literally child's play.

• While the extent of on-line "stalking" and entrapment of children has been exaggerated, such incidents have happened, and parents should monitor children's access to chat rooms. In general, questionable behavior by other users should be reported to the service immediately. Unfortunately, America Online, alone among the major on-line services, allows its users to create a functionally unlimited number of "screen names," or on-line pseudonyms, a policy that seems to have contributed to antisocial behavior on AOL. In fact, America Online has been singled out by child welfare advocates in congressional testimony as being a magnet for pedophiles, at least partially because of its policies on anonymity.

All of the major on-line services have various parental control features that can be used to bar access to certain parts of the services and the Internet, such as chat rooms and objectionable Usenet newsgroups. If you're planning to connect to the Net through an independent Internet service provider (see below), there are programs now available at many software stores (such as Trove Investment Corporation's *Net Nanny* and SurfWatch Software's *SurfWatch*) that can also effectively bar access to certain parts of the Internet. But the ultimate (and only) guarantee of your children's safety on-line is your awareness of what they are doing at all times.

There are many wonderful resources available on-line for children, put there by people who truly love and respect young people and recognize the power of the Net to educate and entertain [see *The Children's Literature Web Guide* (**http://www.ucalgary.ca/~dkbrown**) for example]. The benefits of the Internet are definitely worth the extra time and care it may take to make each child's on-line experience both happy and safe.

Independent Internet Service Providers

The last few years have seen the emergence of an alternative to the major on-line services: independent Internet service providers, or ISPs. ISPs sell access to the Internet, period. Customers dial into an ISP via a modem, and the ISP connects them to the Net. Connecting to the Internet through an ISP has several advantages over connecting through an on-line service like America Online, Prodigy, or CompuServe:

• ISPs are almost always dramatically cheaper than the larger on-line services, at least in part because the trend among ISPs has been to offer untimed, unlimited usage as part of their basic membership plans. A simple "shell" (text-only) account with an ISP costs about $10 per month for unlimited connection time. A more advanced network SLIP/PPP connection (see below) will run from $20 to $30 per month, including anywhere from 40 hours to unlimited time on-line.

• ISPs almost always provide faster, easier access to the Internet than do the on-line services. As a rule, ISPs carry a full Usenet "newsfeed," meaning that users can access any newsgroup they choose, even obscure ones. Other aspects of the Net, such as file transfers, Gopher, and Archie (don't panic—they're all explained in Chapter 3), are also easier and faster to access through ISPs.

• Most ISPs now offer inexpensive SLIP/PPP accounts. A SLIP (Serial-Line Internet Protocol) or PPP (Point-to-Point Protocol, a newer version of SLIP) connection hooks your computer directly into the Internet, making for a substantially faster link than is possible through an on-line service. In addition, a SLIP/PPP connection allows you to use state-of-the-art Internet software (such as the Netscape and Mosaic Web browsers), newsreaders (such as Forte's excellent Agent program), and e-mail programs (such as Qualcomm's Eudora). Best of all, with a SLIP/PPP connection you can pick and choose among hundreds of free or shareware programs available on the Net itself.

• The most dramatic advantage of a SLIP/PPP connection, however, is speed. The difference between viewing a Web page via one of the on-line services' pokey proprietary Web browsers and seeing the same page snap up on your screen in Netscape is breathtaking, and the relief from the chronic slowness of the on-line services' software can make the Internet a far more inviting place to visit.

There are a few factors to consider when deciding whether to use an ISP, especially for newcomers to the on-line world:

• If you're using an on-line service, find it acceptable, and are never running over your quotas of "free" hours, jumping ship to an ISP doesn't make monetary sense. After all, why pay $25 per month for unlimited time if you're only going to use five hours? (If you're using the minimum, you may want to sign up with The WELL, described on page 49, which provides [as of early 1996] five hours per month of full SLIP/PPP Internet access plus The WELL conferences for $15.)

• You should be aware that in opting for an ISP you're giving up the buffer between you and the Net that an on-line service provides. When you connect to an ISP, there is no "there" there—no homey welcome screen, no helpful tips, no on-line customer service department hovering at your elbow, waiting to lead you on a guided tour of the Net. You're simply connected to the Internet in all its glorious anarchy. This can be a disconcerting experience for novices. On the other hand, keep in mind that any reputable ISP will have a help line that you can call with your questions, and if all else fails, the Internet itself is full of folks who love to help newcomers.

• Setting up a SLIP/PPP connection can be more complicated than installing the software for an on-line service. Typically, your new ISP will provide you with disks containing a TCP/IP dialer (pay no attention to all these acronyms—it's really not that complicated), plus rudimentary mail and news programs and a Web browser. Setting up the TCP/IP dialer can be (but usually isn't) a bit tricky. If you're brand-new to computers or modems, make sure that the ISP you choose is willing to walk you through the process of setting up—any reputable ISP will be glad to help.

Depending on where you live, you'll have your choice of anywhere from 1 to 20 local ISPs, plus several national providers. There are good providers and bad providers, and the trick is to separate the two. Word of mouth is probably your best clue: a bad provider gets the reputation it deserves rather quickly. If you already have access to the Internet (via an on-line service or a friend), the best places to find information and opinions about Internet service providers are the **alt.internet.services, alt.internet.access.wanted,** and **alt.online.services** Usenet newsgroups. If you have a question about a specific provider, just post it in one of these groups, and chances are good you'll get an earful, both pro and con.

If you have access to the World Wide Web, there's a very handy Web page called *The List* at **http://www. thelist.com**, which includes nearly all the ISPs in the world, organized by country and area code. Entries for the providers include area codes served, services offered, prices, and telephone numbers. A few minutes spent browsing *The List* will probably produce at least one likely candidate.

If you have no Net access yet, your best bet in finding a local or regional ISP will probably be a quick search of newspaper ads and local bookstores—there are several directories of Internet service providers available.

Another possibility would be to contact a national service provider such as Netcom (800-353-6600), which offers SLIP/PPP connections in most areas of the United States. Netcom accounts come with the service's proprietary software (called Netcruiser), but the Netcom network also allows users to run non-Netcom applications, such as Netscape and the Eudora e-mail program.

Still another possible avenue in finding an ISP would be to invest in one of the ready-made Internet access kits, such as Spry's *Internet In A Box* or NetManage's *Chameleon*, sold in computer software stores and some bookstores. These kits include the software for basic Internet applications (dialing program, World Wide Web browser, e-mail program, etc.), as well as a free trial offer (usually 10 hours or so of on-line time) with a national Internet service provider. If you decide to try one of these kits, make sure that the software can be used with any ISP, not just the one offering the free trial. Although your first few hours on-line with the kit's chosen service provider may be free, dialing into the provider may be a long-distance call for you, which takes most of the fun out of "free." It's also possible, even if accessing the provider is via a local call, that you will consistently get busy signals when you try to dial into the system. But if you first verify that the software can be used with any provider, you can use that free time to find a provider closer to home or less overloaded and switch to it as soon as possible.

The proliferation of local Internet service providers is starting to affect the plans of the large on-line services. Recognizing the superiority of a SLIP/PPP connection over the old-style dial-up hookup, several of the large on-line services are now offering special TCP/IP arrangements that allow users to dial into the service, then run third-party Internet applications such as Netscape alongside the service's proprietary software.

The large on-line services have also decided to give the small local ISPs a run for their money by offering their own bare-bones Internet-only services. America Online, CompuServe, and Prodigy have all established national TCP/IP networks providing full Internet access at rates substantially lower than each service's "full-featured" on-line offerings. Information on these services can be obtained from the phone numbers listed below:

America Online: 800-827-6364
CompuServe: 800-848-8199
Prodigy: 800-PRODIGY

While this sort of account is still usually more expensive than a connection to a local ISP, it may be an option for you if you live in an area without any ISPs at all, and these services' nationwide networks of access numbers make this kind of account an especially attractive option for frequent travelers.

Not to be outdone by the on-line services, both AT&T (800-WORLDNET) and MCI (800-550-0927) now offer Internet access for a low monthly fee, and will soon be joined in the Internet-access business by other national and regional telephone service providers. As a matter of fact, it's probably only a matter of time before your local dry-cleaning establishment will offer to sell you Internet access when you pick up your clothes.

The good news is that, with so much competition in the field, prices for Net access are almost certain to fall in the near future. On the other hand, the volatility of the market means that no guide, not even this one, can keep pace with all the new options for Internet access. But with just a little investigation, chances are good that you'll find an even better deal than the ones I've outlined. You might even get a month's worth of free dry-cleaning in the bargain.

Specialty Providers for Readers and Book Lovers

As the Internet gradually merges into the mainstream of modern life, we can expect to see a dramatic increase in the number of ways to hook up to it. Already the large cable TV companies, telephone companies, and on-line services are wrestling over prime cuts of what promises to be the largest communications cash cow since the invention of movable type. And they all have big plans for the humble little Internet. Someday soon, we're told, the average couch potato will be able to surf the Net on his 64-

inch television from the comfort of his Barcalounger, brewski in one hand, combination remote control and mouse in the other. Television and the Net will merge in "Digital Convergence," we are told—it's inevitable.

Aside from whether such a development is in any way "inevitable" (after all, back in the 1950s it was said to be "inevitable" that we would all own personal helicopters "in a few years"), it is evident that it won't be that simple. The Net has already become many different things to many different groups of people, and a small industry is beginning to emerge based on the market for specialized niche Net access. Some of these services have been around long enough to have built real virtual communities among users who share common interests. We can only hope that these "small towns" along the information superhighway will be spared by the bulldozers of Digital Convergence.

Some of the newer specialized on-line services are aimed at businesses, charge hefty fees for access, and are unlikely to be of interest to individuals living on a fixed budget. These services include sophisticated data search and retrieval services and, in a cheerfully Orwellian marketing ploy, "personal news delivery services" that deliver a customized digital daily "newspaper" composed only of "news" that matches their clients' individual interests. If you actually enjoy the element of surprise inherent in reading your daily newspaper, chances are that such a service is not for you.

At the other end of the spectrum of specialized providers are the broadly based networks, such as PeaceNet, EcuNet, and others catering to a particular spiritual or political constituency. Fees for these services are roughly comparable to those of mainstream on-line services, and details of each service can be found by searching Yahoo (**http://www.yahoo.com**) under either the name of the service, if known, or the general constituency (clergy, activists, etc.) it serves.

As yet, there is no national on-line service specifically tailored for book lovers and readers in general, but if your primary interest on the Internet is serious and informed conversation about books and culture (as well as access to everything on the Internet in general), there is one service that merits consideration—The WELL, based in Sausalito, California.

The WELL was started in 1985 as a local system in the San Francisco Bay Area by the same people who produced *The Whole Earth Catalog* in the late 1960s and 1970s (the name is actually an acronym for "Whole Earth 'Lectronic Link"). Over the years, The WELL has grown into a remarkable on-line community of artists, writers, journalists, poets, and independent thinkers of all trades. At the heart of The WELL are its more than 260 members-only "conferences," or discussion areas, on an amazing variety of topics, ranging from books, writing, media, and poetry to popular culture and UFOs. Discussions on The WELL are lively, well informed, and, in the case of some topics, go on for years. Many of the contributors to The WELL conferences on books and writing are themselves established writers, whose work appears in such magazines as *The New Yorker*, *The Atlantic Monthly,* and *Harper's*—and is often discussed and dissected on The WELL shortly thereafter. The tone of conversations on The WELL is educated and intelligent—a welcome change from what you'll find on the large on-line services and, too often, on the Net in general.

For many years reaching The WELL from outside California required either a long-distance call or a separate Internet account from which one could telnet (log in remotely—see Chapter 3) into the system. Once there, WELL users were faced with a text-only interface that might best be described as idiosyncratic. Recently, however, The WELL established its own national network, offering access to itself and the rest of the Net via SLIP/PPP connections from most major U.S. cities. The WELL has also introduced a World Wide Web interface to its conferencing system, which, although slower than the text system, is much easier for newcomers to master and enjoy. Although the Web interface to the WELL conferences is open to WELL subscribers only, the WELL home page on the Web (**http://www.well.com**) offers descriptions of all the conferences and a good sense of what The WELL is like.

If you already have an Internet connection of some sort, you can access The WELL via either telnet or the Web for $15 per month for unlimited time on-line, an option that I would nominate as the best bargain on the Net. The WELL can be reached at 415-332-9200 or by e-mail at **info@well.com**.

There may be smaller regional conferencing systems or bulletin boards similar to The WELL in your area, so it's worth checking around and possibly asking at your local library. One such system in New York City, Echo, was founded in 1990 and now has approximately 3,000 users and a lively roster of about 50 conferences on various topics going on at any given time. Stacy Horn, the founder of Echo, has been a leading figure in the drive to popularize the on-line world among women, and Echo remains notable among on-line services for the high percentage of women among its users. Being located in Manhattan gives Echo both a particularly "New York" tone and the opportunity to make use of local talent—the "Ms" and "Village Voice" conferences are both hosted by the staffs of those publications. Currently access to Echo from outside the New York area is available only by a long-distance telephone call, unless you already have an Internet connection, in which case, once subscribed to Echo, you can telnet into the system (**telnet://echonyc.com**) from your local Internet account. For more information, Echo can be reached at 212-292-0900 or at **info@echonyc.com**.

Finding the connection to the Internet that best suits your needs and tastes is, ultimately, a process of trial and error. Many Net users who now connect through a SLIP/PPP or even an ISDN link first got their feet wet by subscribing to one of the large on-line services. I myself had accounts with three on-line services and two different Internet service providers before I settled on my current connection (a SLIP/PPP hookup through Interport, a very good ISP in New York City, through which I reach The WELL in California). It's worth shopping around for a good connection, but don't let the wide range of choices get you down—sooner or later you'll end up where you want to be, and you'll have learned a great deal along the way.

Chapter 3

❖

GETTING THERE FROM HERE: THE MANY PATHS THROUGH THE INTERNET

The Internet, like our familiar physical network of roads, carries all sorts of traffic. Most public attention in the last few years has focused on the flashy stretch limo of the infobahn, the World Wide Web with its glamorous graphics. But the Net also has its own lumbering trucks, economy cars, and even bicycles. And just as a charming mountain cabin may be accessible only via a lowly four-wheel-drive vehicle, many of the best spots on the Net can only be reached with some of the older and simpler technologies (stretch limos don't do well on dirt roads, after all). A familiarity with a variety of methods of finding and fetching information can take you off the beaten path to some remarkable things hidden deep in the forests of the Net.

Here, then, is a brief overview of the primary ways to

peek into the nooks and crannies of the Net. In keeping with the nature of this book, I have chosen to make my explanations fairly brief and nontechnical, as there are many sources of more detailed information easily available. Two other methods of information retrieval, Usenet discussion groups and e-mail mailing lists, will be discussed a bit further on, in their own respective chapters.

THE WORLD WIDE WEB AND ITS SEARCH ENGINES

The World Wide Web is the technology primarily responsible for the explosive growth of the Net over the last few years and is probably what most people think of when the Net comes to mind. The Web is the dazzlingly graphic part of the Net—the part that looks like a page in a book or a magazine, usually complete with pictures and fancy layout. When your dentist sends you a postcard telling you that he now has a site on the Internet where you can read all about gum disease, it's a near certainty that he's set up a "home page" on the Web. What makes the current status of the Web as the 500-pound gorilla of the Internet all the more remarkable is that it literally did not exist before 1990, and didn't really get going until 1993. Invented by scientists at the European Particle Physics Laboratory in Switzerland (known as CERN), the Web is a *hypertext information system*, which calls for a little explaining.

Hypertext is a method of linking documents together by means of reference points (called "links," naturally) embedded in the text of each document. Imagine, for example, that I have written a scholarly paper on bats, and at a certain critical point in my article I announce that anyone who doubts my findings should read "page 13 of Professor Rufus T. Firefly's seminal work *Bats Are Me*, available at the National Bat Archives of Freedonia." If I have constructed my paper as a hypertext document and made it available on the Web (and presuming Professor Firefly has done the same), the reader need only click his or her mouse on the highlighted title of the Professor's opus to be instantly transported, not only to the renowned National Bat Archives in far-flung Freedonia, but to the very dissertation in Professor Firefly's extensive oeuvre that proves my point. Hypertext, in theory at least, makes footnotes obsolete.

The Web is essentially a collection (a *very large* collection, mind you) of such hypertext documents linked together. The technology used to navigate among these documents and to bring them to your home computer is known as Hypertext Transfer Protocol, or "HTTP". The revolutionary nature of the Web lies in the power of HTTP to link every document on the Web to every other document without going through any one central directory or menu. Every document or resource on the Web can spawn multiple paths leading in nearly infinite directions directly to other documents—thus the aptness of the "Web" metaphor and name. The Web, like the Internet itself, has no center; any given document (called a "page," stored on a computer at a "Web site"), with its links to other pages around the world, may claim to be the center of the Web with perfect justification. There is no "up" or "down" on the Web; there is only "round and round."

While the development of the Web was a revolution in the organization of information on the Internet, the Web itself didn't really take off in the popular imagination until some folks at the National Center for Supercomputing Applications (NCSA) invented a little program called Mosaic in early 1993. Until Mosaic came along, the Web looked pretty much like everything else on the Net—line after line of text. Mosaic was the first graphic Web browser, and that "graphic" made all the difference. A page on Mosaic, or later graphic browsers such as Netscape, looks like a page in a book or magazine, complete with pictures, fancy type styles, and background colors and textures. Graphic Web browsers also made it much easier to navigate among the myriad interconnected pages of the Web. Hypertext links on a Web page viewed with a graphic browser appear as underlined words or phrases, and once a link is "visited," it will usually appear thereafter underlined in a different color—the high-tech equivalent of trailing a thread to avoid being lost in the labyrinth of the Web.

Mosaic was an immediate hit with Net users, and, more important, with the general public. Millions of home computer users who wouldn't have dared to try to navigate the spartan and confusing "old" Internet were instantly fascinated by Mosaic and the Web. With the advent of the Web and graphic Web browsers, the Internet was finally ready for prime time.

The technology of Web browsers is still evolving at an astoundingly fast pace. The makers of the Netscape browser, in particular, have been instrumental in popularizing a wide range of bells and whistles for Web browsers, such as image maps (pictures coded to take the viewer to various sites when clicked), secure transaction forms (allowing the purchase of goods and services over the Web), and a variety of formatting codes that allow designers to create visually striking Web pages. Consequently, Netscape has become the browser of choice on the Web.

The Web and its graphic browsers have also made it much easier to navigate the non-Web parts of the Internet. Many of the features of the Net that previously were relatively obscure or required mastery of the forbidding Unix interface have been given new legs by the development of goof-proof Web interfaces. It's now far easier to search for and subscribe to a mailing list on a given subject (*Publicly Accessible Mailing Lists*—**http://www.neosoft. com/internet/paml**), or scan all Usenet newsgroup postings for a certain word (*DejaNews Research Service*—**http:// www.dejanews.com**), or locate someone's e-mail address (several methods are available at the *All-in-One Search Page*—**http://www.albany.net/allinone/**) than it used to be, all because these tasks are now possible via simple Web interfaces.

To say that Mosaic, Netscape, and their successors have revolutionized the Web would be like saying that television revolutionized modern life. Graphic Web browsers have proven to be genuine "killer apps"—software applications that make the underlying technology, in this case the Net itself, a "must-have," much as word processing programs drove the original personal computer boom in the 1980s. Within the last three years the number of Web pages on the Net has rocketed from a few hundred to several million. The relatively simple technology required to produce and present a Web page has enabled everyone from telecommunications conglomerates to elementary-school students to put up a page, or two, or a dozen. And, in a sort of hypertext evangelism, nearly every page has at least a few links to other pages, multiplying the possible pathways through the Net several times over.

The lack of hierarchical organization that comes with this infinite number of hypertext links is both the blessing and the curse of the Web. The ability to link resources separated by geography on one page has made it possible to assemble marvelous collections of literature resources from distant universities, for example, or to tie all the major on-line writing workshops together on one handy page. But the decentralized nature of the Web also makes it remarkably difficult to find your way around sometimes—there is, by definition, no one "right" way to get to where you want to go. Hopping from one page to another to another in search of a specific bit of information can be reminiscent of driving aimlessly about an unfamiliar city, often leading to the depressing realization ("Didn't we pass that donut shop a half hour ago?") that you're clicking around in a great big circle.

Search Engines

Enter the search engines and indexes of the Web. The Web was quite young, only a few thousand sites big, when a number of people realized that finding information on the Web was like searching for a needle in a haystack . . . in a hurricane. Web pages came and went (frequently when the college students who created them graduated), entire sites went off-line or simply disappeared, and once the Web really took off, new pages were being added by the hundreds every day. Something had to be done to bring some order to the chaos. There are now a variety of search engines (automated computer programs that scan for a specific term or subject) available on the Web, and while the Web may never be completely organized and indexed (and, after all, it wouldn't be such fun if it were), these search engines can help you get where you want to go.

One of the first, and probably still the most popular, of the Web search engines was Yahoo (**http://www.yahoo. com**), developed by two graduate students in California. To use the Yahoo search engine, you just type in the term or subject you're interested in, click on a "Search" button, and sit back and wait for the results, which will be presented to you as a list of links. You can then click on any one of the links to go to the site Yahoo found for you. If Yahoo itself doesn't find what you're looking for, you can click on links to other search engines and Yahoo will submit your question to them automatically.

The great thing about Yahoo (aside from the fact that it's absolutely free, of course) is that once you're there, you may discover that a search isn't really necessary. The staff of Yahoo spend all of their time maintaining an enormous subject index of the Web in very simple outline form, so what you're looking for may well already have been found and indexed.

Other useful search engines are listed in Chapter 7.

Most of these utilities have options you can use to fine-tune your search (usually there's an "Options" link to click). Narrowing your search with these options will make for a quicker and more productive process.

The Web and Book Lovers

The Web and its rapidly evolving browsers have contributed enormously to the growth of the Net by giving what had been a forbidding text-only network a bright, open, visually appealing look. For the first time, what consumers saw on their computer screens didn't look like something on a computer screen—it looked like a book, or a magazine, or a catalog. And if it *looked* like a book, or a magazine, or a catalog, there was no reason why it couldn't *be* a book, or a magazine, or a catalog. This revolutionary potential of the Web was not lost on print publishers and booksellers, and, not surprisingly, a virtual stampede of booksellers, publishers, magazines, newspapers, writing workshops, and book reviews have rushed onto the Web in the last few years. Today it is a rare publisher or bookstore that does not have at least a minimal presence on the Web, and even small newspapers are scrambling to produce on-line editions for their readers.

One of the most remarkable features of the Web, the ability to link scattered and distant resources to a common page, has proven to be especially popular among book lovers. Almost every page having anything to do with books and reading on the Web, whether created by an individual, a publisher, a bookstore, or a university, is linked to other reading-related resources. The smallest bookstore's home page often carries links to the great libraries of the world, on-line writing groups, and, of course, other lists of reading resources. A virtual visit to a small bookshop in Maine may, within just three or four clicks of your mouse, land you in the Vatican Library or Trinity College in Dublin. And while "location, location, and location" may be the keys to a bookstore's survival in a modern urban setting, physical location and even global geography are irrelevant on the Web, giving a new lease on life to many beleaguered smaller bookshops who now, thanks to their Web pages, have access to a world-wide market. My own home page includes a link to a wonderful bookstore in Galway, Ireland, that I happened to stumble across one day in my Web wanderings.

Even when a Web page focuses on just a single work of one author, hypertext can add several dimensions to the reader's understanding of a book. A hypertext presenta-tion of Jane Austen's *Pride and Prejudice* on the Web (**http://uts.cc.utexas.edu/~ churchh/pridprej.html**) presents Austen's work extensively cross-linked to capsule biographies of every character, genealogical charts ex-plaining the somewhat baroque family relationships in the novel, historical, geographical, and chronological background information for both the story itself and Austen's own life, helpful essays explaining the social conventions of the era, and even illustrations of key mo-ments in the story.

The Web has also led to the development of entirely new kinds of resources for readers that could not have existed before the invention of graphic browsers. Hypertext collaborative novels, diaries, and story projects (see *Madness* at **http://www.channel1.com/users/jay/welcome.htm** for an example), where the reader is invited to contribute to an on-line work-in-progress, are an utterly new feature on the cultural landscape. And conferencing systems (similar to bulletin boards), such as those maintained by *Salon* (**http://www.salon1999.com**) and *Cafe Utne* (**http://www.utne.com**) are, for the first time, allowing readers to talk to each other directly. The result has been the transformation of static print publications into living, dynamic forums for discussion. The truly revolutionary nature of the Web for book lovers may turn out to be the ability it gives us to talk back to the things we read.

GOPHERS IN GOPHERSPACE

While the World Wide Web seems to be getting the lion's share of public attention when it comes to the Internet these days, it has definite limitations. As we've seen, the Web is a remarkably recent invention, while the Net itself has been around since the 1960s. That's a lot of water under the bridge, or, in this case, a lot of material stored on computers around the world before the Web was even thought of. Because of the newness of the Web, and because of the nature of some of the material on the Net, there is an enormous amount of information available on the Internet, some of the "best of the Net," in fact, that does not exist on Web pages.

Welcome to the domain of Gopher. Gopher is an

Internet application that catalogs millions of files residing on computers all over the world and makes them easy to retrieve. Almost all Internet access providers give their users a way to use Gopher. If you use one of the major on-line services, you'll probably find Gopher in the "Internet" area of your service (America Online even has a cute picture of a gopher there to guide its customers). If you access the Net via a SLIP/PPP account with an Internet service provider, your provider will probably give you software for a separate Gopher application to run on your home computer as part of the startup package. If you're operating from a text-only account, look for Gopher under "Internet Applications" on your service's main screen.

A Gopher program will fetch information from the Net and present it in the form of "nested" menus, a menu being a numbered list of items from which to choose. The menus that Gopher presents are nested in that the item you choose from the first list will often lead you to another list, and so on, each of the lists becoming more specific as you home in on your target. You can thus use the menu system of Gopher to "tunnel down" (aha!) to the information you seek, which may be a text file, a graphic, or even a sound file. (In case you missed the point of that "aha!", Gopher's name comes from three sources: (1) it "goes for" information requested by the user by (2) "tunneling" through the Net, and (3) the Gopher program was developed at the University of Minnesota, whose football team is known as the Golden Gophers.)

The Gopher system runs on a network of computers (more than 1,500 of them), called Gopher servers, that are maintained at universities and research facilities throughout the world. Each Gopher server does two things: it catalogs the information within its own domain (its home university, for instance), and it talks to other Gopher servers. Communication between these Gopher servers is the key to Gopher—it gives Gopher the power to transport you instantly to a computer system thousands of miles away if the information you're looking for is likely to be found there. You don't need to know the name of that other computer or where it is; in fact, because Gopher presents everything in the form of uniform text menus, you may not even know you've left one computer for another. Ten items on one menu may represent information located on 10 different computer systems, but Gopher doesn't care—if you want it, just click on it and Gopher takes you there.

Gopher is not a glamorous way to travel the Net. It's pure text and there are none of the bright graphics or dancing icons that litter the Web, for instance. But a few minutes with Gopher will demonstrate its awesome power to find and retrieve information. "Gopherspace"—the sum total of all resources cataloged by all Gopher servers in the world—is composed of millions of documents and files. Libraries, universities, corporations, and foundations make many of their vast resources available via Gopher—reports, essays, reviews, and files that no one would dream of creating a fancy Web page to display, but which might be just what you're looking for. It's often possible to find information of greater depth and sophistication with Gopher than with the Web—technical papers, statistics, research studies, doctoral dissertations, newspaper archives, library catalogs, on-line dictionaries, and much more.

Gopher has two other advantages: it's usually very fast, and it's simplicity itself to operate. Every Gopher system will begin by showing you a basic menu of items from which to choose. One of the most significant choices you'll see on the menu will be called something along the lines of "Other Gopher and Information Servers." This item is your ticket to the world of Gopherspace. Click on this item and you'll be presented with another list, on which will appear an item labeled "All the Gopher Servers in the World," and, yes, they're serious. Take this route and you'll be presented with a long list of Gopher servers arranged by continent and country. If you're looking for information on Malaysia, for example, you've hit the mother lode with just three clicks—not bad at all. Another item will be labeled "Gopher Jewels." Click on this and you'll be met with a handy menu of major categories of information, such as "law," "literature," "medicine," and "humor." Each of these items will take you deeper into lists devoted to that particular subject. Feel free to explore, and don't worry about getting lost. Fortunately, Gopher programs usually give you a way to create "bookmarks" that will help you to develop a list of favorite places to visit in Gopherspace.

A Visit From Veronica

If Gopher has a disadvantage, it may be that while you can easily go "up" and "down" within the tunnels you dig, you cannot go "across" to the middle of another tunnel. If you realize at some point in a search for information that you're headed down a dead end, you'll have to go back at least a few menus before you can start your search again on a different path. Another problem with Gopher is that you can't tell whether what you want is at a certain place until you get there, a process sometimes reminiscent of, but often less rewarding than, going trick-or-treating door-to-door as a child. Some houses just give you apples, and others don't answer the door at all.

Both of these problems are addressed by a program you'll find in Gopherspace called Veronica. The name stands for (pay attention, because you'll be able to impress your friends by knowing this) Very Easy Rodent-Oriented Net-wide Index to Computerized Archives, and yes, the "rodent" is Gopher. Veronica is a search engine that will comb Gopherspace for any term you specify, going door-to-door for you, and return a menu of links or files containing that term. You then simply click on the links to view the files that Veronica has found, thereby saving yourself the trouble of tracking them down by trial and error. Finding Veronica itself is no problem at all—you'll see invitations to "Search Gopherspace with Veronica" on most major Gopher menus you'll encounter. You'll probably even have a choice of Veronica locations from which to search. If a Veronica search at one location doesn't produce what you're looking for, you can always try one somewhere else. Be sure to read the "How to Compose Veronica Queries" file that you'll find listed next to Veronica, by the way. There are a number of ways to fine-tune your Veronica searches that will make them faster and more productive.

Even if you never actually set out to use Gopher, you'll probably run across it in your travels on the

Web. Most Web browsers can view Gopher menus, and it's becoming increasingly common to find links between Web sites and Gopher resources. If you're looking for something on the Web and come across a Gopher menu, jump right in. As a repository of heavy-duty down-and-dirty specialized information, Gopher-space is hard to beat, and probably will be for a long time to come.

WAIS

One of the limitations of Gopher is that while it can uncover (with Veronica's help) remarkable sources of information, Gopher can only judge a book, or a file, by its cover. Ask Veronica to find information on Dickens, for instance, and you'll probably get back a list of a hundred or more links and files, all with the word "Dickens" in the title. But what Veronica won't find are files that mention Dickens in some regard but don't happen to have the word "Dickens" in the title. Veronica's weakness in this respect might well lead it (her?) to overlook, among other things, articles detailing Dickens's influence on subsequent novelists.

Into this rather disturbing gap steps WAIS (pronounced "ways"), which stands for Wide Area Information Server. WAIS is remarkable in that it is a *full-text* search engine. To milk the metaphor a bit, if Veronica only glances at the cover of a book in judging whether to fetch it for you, WAIS sits down and reads the whole book before deciding. Of course, WAIS doesn't really scan entire texts every time you ask a question; it depends on databases composed of the full texts of hundreds of sources, already indexed and cross-referenced. WAIS is also capable of ranking the information it returns to you in order of relevance to your query. But WAIS doesn't stop there—if it brings back answers that are in the ballpark but not precisely what you had in mind, just note the answers that are closest to the mark and WAIS will go back and search again based on your refined query. Running a WAIS search is like having your own personal research assistant trotting around the Internet for you.

WAIS has its limitations, of course. Its databases are not encyclopedic, and if what you're looking for hasn't been indexed in a WAIS database, WAIS won't find it. On the other hand, WAIS is free and easy to operate, so if you haven't found what you're looking for using other search methods, WAIS is certainly worth a shot. Like Gopher, WAIS programs can run either on a host computer (at an on-line service, for example) or on your home machine (if you have a SLIP/PPP connection). You may even run across a WAIS connection as a menu item in the course of a Gopher search, giving you the opportunity to simply input your search subject and initiate a WAIS search then and there.

ARCHIE

In case you were wondering why anyone would bother to dream up a convoluted acronym to name a simple program "Veronica" (see above), here's your answer: remember the comic strip? Veronica was Archie's girlfriend in the comics, and before there was Veronica (the search program), there was Archie, a program that locates specific files, usually computer programs, on the Internet. The key word here is "specific": to succeed in an Archie search, you must know at least part of the name of the file you're looking for. Archie will not search for general topics or keywords.

Like Gopher and WAIS searches, Archie searches can be run either from a program on your own computer (if you have a SLIP/PPP account) or via an on-line service. Archie searches can be most productive when you're looking for a specific program (a digital encryption program, for instance) and you know the exact filename (pgp262.zip). If you're not sure about the name of the program, or if you just want to browse through programs of a certain type, you'll be better off checking out one of the many shareware archives on the Web (Jumbo, at **http://www.jumbo.com**, is a good place to start).

FTP

Sooner or later, you're going to want to download something from the Internet. "Downloading" is the process of copying a file from a remote computer to your own home computer so that you can read it, work with it, or, if the file is a program, install and run it. Perhaps you'd like the latest version of Netscape—after all, the company seems to release a new one just about every week.

Or perhaps you've always wanted a digitized version of *Moby Dick* (but you'd better wait until the weekend— downloading the whole book could easily take all day).

Every on-line service has its own file libraries and download mechanisms, but out on the wild and woolly Internet almost all file transfers are handled by a method called FTP (file transfer protocol). FTP is a very powerful and flexible method of transporting and managing files on the Net—not only can you download files to your own computer, but you can also upload files from your home machine onto a remote computer. If you establish a personal home page on the Web (see Chapter 6), for example, you'll probably use an FTP program to put up and periodically update the page.

As is the case with Gopher, Archie, and other programs described above, you'll be using FTP either through an interface supplied by an on-line service or through an FTP program running on your home computer via a SLIP/PPP connection. Most SLIP/PPP accounts will include a basic FTP utility as part of the startup package, and more sophisticated FTP programs are available as shareware on the Net itself. Many Web browsers, such as Netscape, can also handle FTP transfers automatically.

The most common use of FTP programs is to copy files from a remote computer (known as an "FTP site") by means of a procedure known as "Anonymous FTP." In Anonymous FTP, you're actually logging into a remote computer (using the word "anonymous" as your login name and your e-mail address as your password) and copying files to your own system. If you're using

FTP through an on-line service, you won't have to worry about a login and password: the on-line service's system will take care of that for you. If you're using an FTP program on your home computer, just check the "anonymous" box in the configuration dialog box and you'll be in business.

To transfer files from an FTP site to your home computer, you'll need to know both the name of the file you're looking for and the exact directory in which it resides on the host computer. Fortunately, most magazine articles or Internet sites that mention a program or file that you might want to FTP will also give you the information you'll need in a standard addressing format—**ftp://ftp.twinkies.com/pub/neatstuff.txt**—or something similar. In this example, you'd FTP to the "ftp.twinkies.com" site, switch to the "pub" directory (which is where files available to the public are stored on many computer systems), then look around for a file called "neatstuff.txt." Just tell your FTP program where you want that file stored on your home computer, hit the "file transfer" button, and the rest is usually automatic.

FTP is one of the core applications on the Internet, and it's definitely worth the few minutes it may take you to master it. Besides allowing you to take advantage of the vast software resources available on the Net, FTP can fetch some of the best written resources on the Net. Any sort of long text file, whether a dissertation, technical report, or novella, will probably be too long to be found on a Web site or in a newsgroup, and it may not be available via Gopher or WAIS. In cases like these, a basic familiarity with FTP will not only allow you to zip in and grab the file, but after downloading it to your home computer, will give you plenty of time to read the file off-line (especially important if you're paying on-line service time charges).

Two caveats apply to using FTP, however. First, remember that whenever you're connected to a remote computer system you're a guest there and that, in all likelihood, the system was intended for use by people doing serious work. If possible, conduct FTP sessions after business hours (whatever they may be where the host computer system is located).

Second, while there is almost no chance of accidentally acquiring a computer virus by downloading software from a corporate site or from one of the major shareware libraries on the Net, it's still wise to use a good antivirus scanning program before you run any program. Text and graphics files, on the other hand, pose no threat of viruses—viruses can only be transmitted in a program file.

TELNET

Telnet is one of the oldest applications on the Net and still one of the most versatile. When you "telnet into" a site, you're actually logging onto that computer as a user—what you see on your home computer screen is exactly what a local user on that remote system would see. Most often, you'll be presented with a text-only menu when you telnet into a system. If you're accessing the system through an on-line service or other graphic interface, a separate window will open up, usually showing white text on a black background, and a blinking cursor. Don't be alarmed; you'll always see instructions about how to log onto, as well as how to exit from, the remote system.

Telnet may not be the most glamorous method of getting information on the Net, but it is one of the most powerful, and there are some very neat things on the Net reachable only via telnet. Many library catalogs, for instance, are accessible only by telnet—the library itself may have a very impressive Web page with stately graphics and basic information, but if you want to know if it has a particular book or journal, you'll end up using telnet to find out. Telnet is also useful when you subscribe to a faraway bulletin board or conferencing system that does not have free local phone numbers in your area. Rather than calling long-distance to my account on The WELL, a system in California, for example, I can telnet in from my local New York provider, thus paying only the cost of a local call. (In this case, I could also use The WELL's own national network, but that's a bit more expensive.)

The particulars of how to access and use telnet will vary according to how you access the Internet, but the telnet system itself is refreshingly simple, and, once you get the hang of it, you'll find it to be one of the quickest and handiest ways to hop around the Net.

IRC (INTERNET RELAY CHAT)

Most of the Internet is "time-shifted"—while people communicate in a variety of ways over the Net, the messages are rarely transmitted and received in real time (i.e., simultaneously), as on a telephone. You post a message to me in a Usenet discussion group (see Chapter 4) or send an e-mail. I read your message the next day and send a reply, which you then read later that day or next week. A Web page may exist on the Net for weeks or months before anyone sees it (if ever), and many of the files accessible by Gopher have been snoozing peacefully on their home systems for years. For a cutting-edge system of communication, the Internet actually carries on its business at a remarkably pastoral (some would say glacial) pace.

There is an analogue of the telephone on the Net, however, that lets you talk (albeit by typing on your keyboard) to anyone who happens to be on-line at the same time, anywhere in the world. Internet Relay Chat (IRC) is a global real-time system of hundreds of channels, each with its own topic, on which thousands of people can "chat" with each other 24 hours a day. For many years, IRC was restricted to only the most technically proficient Net users by virtue of a confusing interface and arcane operating commands. Recently, however, a new generation of user-friendly IRC software (such as Khaled Mardam-Bey's "freeware" mIRC for the Windows operating system and Netscape Chat for a range of operating systems) has opened the world of IRC to newcomers to the Net.

IRC is enormously popular, as are the "chat rooms" (similar to IRC) maintained by all of the large on-line services for their users. The on-line services have acknowledged that most of their revenue comes from users' racking up hourly charges using the services' chat rooms, and it is not unusual to find more than 1,000 IRC channels open and operating on any given evening on the Net.

Unfortunately, IRC sounds like a much more exciting place than it actually is. The level of discourse found there (and even more so in the on-line services' chat rooms) is relentlessly inane, often pointlessly obscene, and, worst of all, mind-numbingly boring. One newspaper reporter, after exploring the America Online chat rooms for a while, remarked that Dante, had he lived in the 1990s, would not have given his vision of Hell "rings"—he'd have given it "chat rooms."

There are, of course, exceptions, even on IRC. Pick a channel called "Friendly," "Pub," or "Callahans," and you'll meet a group of very nice regulars discussing a variety of topics. The folks on the "Over 40" channel tend to be kinder and gentler than the rest of IRC's denizens. There's even a channel called "Writers," devoted to chat about writing, although, because of the fundamental incoherence of IRC, sustained conversations of substance are very rare.

It's all a matter of opinion, of course, and to each his or her own. Evidently some people find IRC and chat rooms fascinating enough to have made the on-line services very rich (and to have necessitated the formation of a Usenet newsgroup called "alt.irc.recovery" to help wean IRC addicts). If, however, you have ever wished for a few extra hours in the day so that you could catch up with your reading, you're unlikely to be tempted to spend any substantial amount of time on IRC.

Chapter 4

USENET DISCUSSION GROUPS: ADDING YOUR TWO CENTS' WORTH

Much of the Internet is essentially a passive, solitary medium. Popular phrases such as "surfing the Net" may conjure up visions of acrobatic hotdogging, but the truth is that the average Net surfer's physical exertions amount to no more than clicking a mouse or typing a few terse commands and watching the results pop up on the computer screen. In most cases, there is no one home at the other end of that network connection: the Web page or FTP site resides on a remote computer, running unattended, delivering the same content hour after hour with all the warmth and personality of a soft-drink machine. Much as Netters might like to think otherwise, sitting in front of a computer, clicking a mouse button, bears a disquieting resemblance to sitting in front of a television set, clicking a remote control. (Alone, yet. While communal television viewing provides an opportunity for at least some, albeit low-quality, socializing, very few families outside of computer ads actually gather 'round the ol' Pentium on a winter's evening.) The worst-case scenario of the explosive growth of the Internet over the last few years, heard with increasing frequency from critics of the Net, is that the entire on-line revolution brouhaha will ultimately breed a nation of "Net potatoes," vast herds of passive browsers wedded to their computers, cut off from all contact and conversation with real people as they click their way from site to site, caught in a Web of solitude.

If this dystopian view of the Internet and the on-line world does not come to pass, it will be largely thanks to that part of the Internet known as Usenet, perhaps the most exuberantly anarchic experiment in collective free speech in human history. Freedom of the press may belong, as the cynics say, to those who own the presses, but the beauty (and the genuinely revolutionary nature) of Usenet is that it gives anyone with a computer and a network connection the equivalent of not just a printing press, but a built-in worldwide audience of millions of readers.

Thanks to Usenet, I can roust myself out of bed at 3 A.M., compose a masterful analysis of the socioeconomic significance of the recent public fascination with the works of Jane Austen, post it to the relevant newsgroup (**rec.arts.books**) in a matter of five seconds or so, and crawl back into bed with the satisfaction of knowing that before noon the next day somewhere between several thousand and several million people will have read (or at least glanced at) my masterpiece. Usenet gives anyone with an Internet connection an ability to broadcast his or her opinion to the world unmatched by even the largest newspaper and television networks.

And broadcast we will. While it's possible to just sit back and watch Usenet scroll by, sooner or later everyone feels the overwhelming need to contribute his or her two cents' worth to the thousands of ongoing discussions that make up Usenet. The art of conversation is alive and well on Usenet.

WHAT IS USENET?

Begun in the infancy of the Internet in 1979 as a way for Unix computer programmers and a few academics to share information over the fledgling network, Usenet (known originally as "Netnews") today encompasses over 14,000 different "newsgroups," each of which acts as a bulletin board devoted to a particular topic. (Occasionally you may hear an old-timer proclaim that Usenet is "not part of the Internet." Technically speaking, this is true, in that some sites that are not connected to the Internet do receive Usenet material.)

Although Usenet is made up of "newsgroups", there is very little of what most of us would consider "news" in the conventional sense on Usenet. But there are plenty of personal opinions—and opinions, often strongly held, are the essence of Usenet. Consequently, there are newsgroups devoted to nearly every topic anyone might have an opinion on, from cats to opera to poetry to mysticism to baseball to car repair. Within a given newsgroup, messages are posted on a variety of topics (called "threads"), most of which, on a good day, have something to do with the overall theme of the newsgroup. Any user who reads a posting (also called an "article") on a particular topic and has something to say on the subject can then reply to the first posting, or to someone else's reply, and so on, ad infinitum. Any user can also start a brand-new thread and then sit back and watch over the next few days as fellow Netters agree, disagree, or simply ignore the topic entirely. Replies are likely to roll in from around the world, and often in astonishing numbers. While low-traffic newsgroups may receive only 5 or 10 contributions per day, some of the more popular often see between 300 and 500 new postings every day of the week—quite a change from the early days of Netnews, when the design specifications for the system that was to become Usenet estimated that the traffic would be a total of two articles per day.

Perhaps the most remarkable characteristic of Usenet is that, by and large, no one is in charge. Any article posted to a newsgroup is rapidly transmitted from the author's host system to thousands of computers (called "news servers") all over the world, each of which stores the article and makes it available to the users of that local system. There is, therefore, no "Usenet Central" that can pull the plug on opinions it finds offensive—with rare exceptions, no one can erase an article from the worldwide Usenet system except the author of that particular article.

That Usenet lacks a "master control" does not mean that anarchy prevails, however. Usenet has developed a singular communal culture over the years, complete with its own traditions, standards, folklore, and lingo. Not surprisingly, the users of Usenet have also collectively developed principles of netiquette (see Chapter 1 for an explanation of netiquette) spelling out what constitutes unacceptable on-line behavior. Posting advertisements in inappropriate newsgroups (there are newsgroups set aside for this purpose), excessive "flaming" (posting insulting or obscene messages), posting messages having nothing to do with the topic of the newsgroup (lobbing singles ads into the **rec.pets.cats** newsgroup, for instance), and a few other notable transgressions are all violations of netiquette. Netiquette is informal but almost universally observed, and the penalties for violations range from flaming the offender to, if the offender is being seriously and consistently disruptive, complaining to whoever provides the offender's Net access (on-line service, university system administrator, etc.). If any access provider receives more than a few complaints about a given user, that user's access is almost certain to be yanked. Such a drastic solution is a rare occurrence, largely because Usenet users across the political spectrum are, almost without exception, passionate defenders of free speech. It also helps the cause of tolerance that most good newsreading programs (see page 83) contain a feature called a "killfile," which enables a user to ignore posts from known "Net kooks."

If you want your debut in Usenet to be auspicious, you'll want to spend some time reading the postings in the newsgroup created just to help newcomers get their bearings, called, logically enough, **news.announce.newusers**. If you have questions about Usenet or any other part of the Internet, post them in **news.newusers.questions**, and you'll probably get answers from all over the Net.

THE ORGANIZATION OF USENET NEWSGROUPS

The prospect of browsing through over 14,000 Usenet newsgroups to find just the ones dealing with your favorite topics of discussion may seem a little daunting, but don't worry. Newsgroups are organized into a remarkably logical (again, considering that no one is "in charge") hierarchy. The hierarchy is composed of eight main groups, each of which has numerous subgroupings, reflected in the names of the individual newsgroups. Seven of the top-level groups are considered the original, "official" Usenet categories:

comp.	computer-related
misc.	miscellaneous and unclassifiable topics
news.	Usenet and the Internet
rec.	recreational (hobbies, art, music, etc.)
sci.	science-related
soc.	social issues
talk.	general discussion on a variety of topics

Each top-level domain is divided into a family tree of groups, whose lineage can be discerned by the logical arrangement of their names, reading from left to right as they become more specialized. For example:

rec.arts.music
rec.arts.music.classical
rec.arts.music.classical.recordings

This branching-tree approach lends a welcome order to what otherwise would be a chaotic assortment of groups.

In the eighth top-level grouping are the "alt." (or "alternative") newsgroups, the domain of the wild, the wacky, and the often just plain strange. The alt. groups comprise the "unofficial" Usenet groups, and they differ from the original seven top-level groupings in several ways. The most notable is that while there are standardized and fairly rigorous procedures involved in starting an "official" newsgroup (involving public petitioning and voting, all taking place on Usenet, of course), anyone can start an alt. group. All that a prospective founder of an alt. group (say, Joe Smith) need do is convince enough system administrators to carry the new group (alt.fan.joe-smith, most likely) on their news servers. The upside of this open-door policy is that it has led to the creation of some of the liveliest groups on Usenet—alt.folklore.urban and alt. usage.english, for instance, to name two of my favorites. The downside of the ease with which alt. groups can be set up can be seen in groups such as "alt.tv. dinosaurs.barney.die.die.die." (not to mention "alt.sex. bestiality.barney") and the consequent refusal of many system administrators (especially at universities) to carry the alt.* hierarchy of groups. Many on-line services do not include the alt.* hierarchy in their basic newsgroup offerings, although most will let you read them if you already know the name of the group. Most of the independent Internet service providers, in contrast, carry a full newsfeed (i.e., all 14,000-plus Usenet groups, including the entire alt.* hierarchy) and allow their subscribers to make their own decisions on matters of taste and morality.

Depending on the range of newsgroups your particular provider carries, you will occasionally see groups beginning with odd letters, such as **ny.** and **az.** These are geographically or institutionally local newsgroups mostly of interest to the people who live in that particular area or attend a particular school. My Internet service provider in New York City, for instance, not only carries the "**nyc.**" groups but also, for some inexplicable reason, newsgroups in the "**oh.*** " hierarchy, pertaining to Ohio. On a more useful note, a really good provider will carry the ClariNet newsgroup hierarchy (**clari.***), a commercial service that posts actual news from the Associated Press and other sources, in the form of Usenet articles.

Most providers also maintain internal Usenet groups, usually in a hierarchy beginning with the service's name ("interport.questions," "interport.announce," etc.). These groups are only visible to users of that particular provider, are usually monitored by the service provider itself, and can be a valuable source of information if you have questions about either the service or the Internet in general.

The vast majority of Usenet groups aren't moderated: anyone can post anything without fear of censorship or reprisal (except the possibly negative reactions of other users of the group). A few newsgroups, by common agreement among their users, are moderated; any posting automatically goes first to a moderator, who decides whether it is relevant to the purpose of the group. If it is, the moderator then forwards it to the general newsfeed for distribution. Moderated newsgroups have a higher signal-to-noise ratio than unmoderated groups but often pay a penalty in dullness.

Usenet being the remarkably self-organized place that it is, there is an information desk for nearly every newsgroup—the Frequently Asked Questions file, or FAQ—where newbies can get the lowdown on the theme, history, quirks, and quibbles of the group and its regular contributors before plunging in. Reading the FAQ for a group before posting there is one of the most important ground rules of netiquette and the best way to avoid making a bad first impression on the locals. Most Usenet groups regularly post their FAQs in the group itself every month or so, but a wide variety of FAQs are also always available at **ftp://ftp.rtfm.mit.edu/pub/ usenet**. The "rtfm," by the way, stands for an old hacker catchphrase: "Read the (friendly, freakin', whatever) manual." It's good advice. Reading the FAQ will prove invaluable in helping you to avoid being roasted and toasted by flames on your first foray into a newsgroup.

NEWSREADERS

The program used to read messages on Usenet (and to write and post your own) is called a newsreader. There are a wide variety of newsreaders in use on the Net, ranging in quality and ease of use from the ridiculous to the sublime, but the type of newsreader you will end up using will largely be determined by how you access the Net. All newsreaders allow you to "subscribe" to certain groups that you plan to read regularly; the other 13,985 (or whatever) groups are then hidden from sight, so you don't have to scroll through them every day to get to your favorites.

On-line services such as America Online, Prodigy,

and CompuServe include newsreading software in their all-in-one proprietary software suites, often hidden behind a button that calls Usenet by another name, such as "Internet Bulletin Boards" or "Discussion Groups." Most newsreaders of this type come preconfigured with a few startup newsgroups, leaving it up to the user to pick additional groups to read. Some groups, especially those in the alt.* hierarchy, are often not listed in the service's master list of available groups, although they can usually be added if you already know the exact name of the group you want to read.

Unfortunately (and ironically, since these services stress ease of use as a selling point), the newsreading software supplied by on-line services is almost always slow and awkward. It often also lacks basic features, such as quoting parts of the message you're replying to, forwarding a posting via e-mail, and sending the same message to more than one group (called "cross-posting"). If you're starting out on an on-line service and find Usenet a valuable and enjoyable resource, keep in mind that one of the advantages of eventually switching to an Internet service provider with a SLIP/PPP connection is the ability to use one of the vastly superior TCP/IP newsreaders on the market.

If you're accessing the Net through a university, freenet, Unix, or other text-based account, the newsreader you use will be dictated by the tastes of the person administering your system, since the newsreading software runs on the host computer, not your personal machine. The bad news is that whatever newsreader you are offered (probably a Unix program called TIN, RN, or

TRN) will be strictly text-based and not very pretty to look at. The good news is that it will be much faster, more powerful, and (once you get the hang of it) easier to use than the newsreaders offered by the on-line services. Many experienced users with access to graphic newsreaders still prefer to use TIN or TRN.

If you're connecting to the Net through a direct network or SLIP/PPP dial-up connection, the world is your oyster, newsreader-wise. Depending on the type of computer you're using, there is a wide variety of TCP/IP newsreader software, both commercial and shareware, available on the Internet itself. Most providers include a basic newsreader in their startup software packages for new customers, but these newsreaders are often older shareware versions. Finding a better newsreader is just a matter of logging onto the Net, seeking out one of the many shareware libraries on-line, and taking your pick. (Yahoo at **http://www.yahoo.com** is a good place to start.)

Another newsreading route for the direct-network or SLIP/PPP user is the "suite" or "Swiss Army Knife" software package. Like the proprietary software of the on-line services, the packages combine several functions (Web browser, mail client, FTP, etc.) in one ornate program and usually contain some sort of newsreader. Unfortunately, these programs tend to suffer from the same woes that afflict the on-line services' software: slowness and substandard features. Still, the all-in-one approach has enormous popular appeal (and consequently is a high priority for software developers), so keep an eye out for improvements in this area. Current versions of the

Netscape browser include a newsreader, which works fairly well but is not the equal of standalone applications such as Agent.

One of the most welcome features now becoming popular in well-designed newsreaders is an off-line capability. Rather than forcing the user to read news-groups while on-line (and often racking up per-hour charges), a newsreader with this feature allows the user to log on, automatically grab all of the headers (sub-ject/author/date lines) of articles in favorite newsgroups, then log off. The user can leisurely review the headers in each group, pick the ones that sound interesting, and log back on just long enough to allow the newsreader to grab the bodies of the chosen articles. An off-line newsreader can dramatically cut the cost of reading Usenet news-groups, as well as allowing you to read articles days or weeks after they are posted (by which time the article it-self would probably have expired on the news server and no longer be available).

NEWSGROUPS OF PARTICULAR INTEREST TO READERS

With more than 14,000 Usenet newsgroups to choose from, anyone who attempts to read even just those groups that initially sound interesting will be quickly overwhelmed by the sheer volume of postings. Most people end up subscribing to and regularly reading per-haps 7 to 10 groups on a regular basis. What follows is a list of a few of my favorites. They don't all relate directly to books or reading, but they're all worth checking out at least occasionally. Many more newsgroups related to books are listed in Chapter 7.

rec.arts.books

This newsgroup is home base for book lovers on the Net. Traffic in the group is brisk, with between 50 and 100 new postings every day. The discussion topics range from "books set in cold locations—recommendations?" to debates over the possibly deleterious effects of "book superstores" such as Barnes & Noble. The only constants in this group seem to be debates about the works of Ayn Rand and censorship. Most important book-related FAQs are periodically posted here.

bit.listserv.literary

Similar to **rec.arts.books** in many ways, this is a Usenet redistribution of an academic e-mail mailing list and may not be available at some sites. The tone here tends to be a bit heavier, more serious and academic, than that in **rec.arts.books**.

misc.writing

Ain't nobody here but us writers . . . by the hundreds. All sorts of writers, from successful freelancers to aspiring novelists to closet journal keepers, check in here to swap tips on writing, agents, contracts, and copyright law. If you want to be a writer but lack confidence, this is the place to come; probably the most supportive folks on the planet hang out here.

alt.usage.english

Ever wonder where the word "posh" came from? Unsure about the placement of a period with quotation marks? Can't seem to remember what a participle is? Stay up late at night wondering what people in different countries call the strip of grass in the middle of a highway? Here you'll find the answers, along with extended debates on nearly every conceivable issue of English language usage. A high-traffic group, **alt.usage.english** also boasts an extensive and fascinating FAQ updated and posted monthly by Mark Israel.

alt.folklore.urban

Is someone in your office collecting soda can pop-tops for a fund to buy a kidney dialysis machine? Is your best friend encouraging you to send hundreds of get-well cards to a sick boy in England so the lad can get into the *Guinness Book of World Records*? Did a friend of a friend bite into a frog lurking in her taco at a fast-food restaurant? Get thee to **alt.folklore.urban** (also known as AFU), where the mythology of modern life meets its debunkers. One of the more popular groups on Usenet, AFU is home to some of the smartest and funniest regulars on the Net, but they don't suffer fools gladly, so be sure to read the FAQ before posting.

There's also a moderated and thus more "serious" relative of **alt.folklore.urban**, called **alt.folklore.suburban** (the "suburban" connoting a subsidiary relationship to the "urban" group, not a fixation on lawn furniture), where the discussion is governed by the tastes of the moderator. Whether exploding poodles and bizarre suicides really deserve this level of serious discussion, of course, is open to question.

alt.folklore.ghost-stories

All ghost stories, all the time—a sort of 24-hour spook channel on the Net. Here you'll find personal accounts of encounters with somewhat transparent former relatives. It's guaranteed to give even hardened skeptics the wimwams.

alt.humor.best-of-usenet

The funniest messages from the Usenet are helpfully reposted here for your convenience. The quality varies but every so often a true not-to-be-missed classic (such as the famous "Microsoft Buys Catholic Church" announcement) crops up.

soc.history.what-if

What if the Japanese had won World War II? What if President Kennedy hadn't been assassinated? What if Bill Gates hadn't been born, or had been born a girl, or born a goldfish? Welcome to the wonderful world of what if, where hypotheticals flourish and you can let your urge to speculate off the leash and watch it run barking into the woods. Most of the discussion here centers on wars, revolutions, and other cataclysmic events, not surprisingly, but at least the history lessons are never dull. Relentlessly strange, but not dull.

alt.conspiracy

Not a group that anyone should read too closely, but an occasional visit will make you feel rock-solid sane in comparison to some of the folks who hang out here. Mysterious black helicopters, alien abductions, and Microsoft's plans for world domination are all fodder for the nut mill. Most likely the only group on the Net where a thread entitled "The Hollow Earth Theory Is Probably a Hoax" (*probably?*) would prompt a string of serious replies.

alt.politics.correct

Put out that cigarette and pay attention, fascist dog. If you happen to be suffering from low blood pressure, this newsgroup is just the ticket. Left and Right unite in a nonstop paranoid mud-wrestling marathon. This newsgroup features extended debates on Rush Limbaugh's parentage and is best in small doses—just reading the subject lines in this group is enough to tick off most people.

alt.fan.cecil-adams

This is a newsgroup devoted to discussing "The Straight Dope," a syndicated newspaper column that answers such age-old questions as "Where are all the baby pigeons?" and "Why do monopolies bother to advertise?" This is a remarkably civil group, homey and pleasant to read.

comp.internet.net-happenings

Lo and behold, here's a newsgroup that actually contains news. It's one of the best ways to stay abreast of new developments on the Net, especially new mailing lists, e-zines, and Web sites. This is a high-traffic, one-way group (no posting except by the moderator, an incredibly hardworking fellow named Gleason Sackman).

humanities.lit.authors.shakespeare

This is one of the first groups established in the new "humanities" hierarchy. This is a low-traffic group at the moment, but it will probably take off as more sites begin to carry such groups. Besides, if Anne Rice gets a newsgroup, surely there's room for the Bard.

news.newusers.questions

If you're new to the Net, this is the place to ask nearly any question. If you've been around for a while, it's always nice to stop by and answer a few questions. Besides, you'll probably learn something useful yourself.

alt.society.neutopia

Doctress Neutopia (also known as Libby Hubbard) is a sometime graduate student at the University of Massachusetts and author of a (choose one) (a) charmingly idealistic, (b) fundamentally impractical, or (c) clearly demented theory of how to build a new utopian ("Neutopian") society. It's a very long story. This newsgroup not only provides the good Doctress a platform for her, um, pronouncements but gives her beer-swilling nemeses (known as the Monster Truck Neutopians) a place to post their recipes for barbecue sauce. This group definitely wins the Down-the-Rabbit-Hole Award and has to be read to be believed.

FINDING INFORMATION ON USENET

Just because Usenet doesn't contain very much "hard news" doesn't mean it can't be an extremely useful source of information. Newsgroups devoted to a particular topic are some of the best sources of information on that topic, since, by definition, the "regulars" in a given group are passionately interested in the topic of the group. On occasion, I have found excellent information about dictionaries of rhyming slang in **alt.usage.english**, helpful explanations of some of the more arcane rituals of the English ruling class in **alt.fan.wodehouse**, and a source for a biography of the Irish humorist Flann O'Brien in **rec.arts.books**. Most regulars in a given group are eager to answer questions about the group's topic (provided that you have checked the group's FAQ for the answer first—no one enjoys answering the same questions over and over).

One caveat: Take everything you read on Usenet with several grains of salt. Chances are that you'll receive more than one reply to any question you post, and it's up to you to decide whom, if anyone, to trust. *Never rely on Usenet for answers to medical, legal, or financial questions*, and be very skeptical about any advice regarding computers that may be offered.

With that in mind, the trick is to find the proper group in which to ask your question. You could scroll through a list of all 14,000 newsgroups, if you have the patience, and take a stab at the more likely groups. Or you could zip over to *The Liszt of Newsgroups* page (yes, it's a silly pun) on the World Wide Web at **http://www.liszt.com/cgi-bin/news.cgi**. Just enter the topic you're searching for, click on the button, and in a moment a sophisticated search engine will present you with a list of newsgroups meeting your criteria. If you're using Netscape or another browser with an integrated newsreading feature, clicking on the name of a newsgroup will take you right there and you can begin your reading at once. *The Liszt of Newsgroups* page, by the way, is linked to another page called *The Liszt of Lists* (somebody out there really likes that pun), where you can run the same sort of search to find the names and addresses of mailing lists on a given subject.

Another way to search Usenet is offered by *The Deja News Search Page* (yes, yet another corny pun) at **http://www.dejanews.com/forms/dnquery.html**. Here you simply type in a word or words to search for, hit the button, and wait for the search engine to present you with a list of articles, fetched from every group on Usenet, containing those words. You can also customize your search by date, number of results, or other criterion. One interesting (and mildly Orwellian) use of the Deja News service is to search for postings by a particular person—the search engine will show you every posting by that person in every group over the last few months.

STARTING A NEWSGROUP

So you've sifted through all 14,000 Usenet newsgroups and discovered that, as unbelievable as it seems, there is no group devoted to the work of your favorite author. No *alt.fan.flann-obrien* ! No *alt.fan.sj-perelman* ! No *alt.fan.winthrop-fortescue*! (Who?) In any case, it's an outrage, and it's up to you to rectify the oversight. What to do? Simple: Start the newsgroup yourself.

Starting a Usenet newsgroup may seem to be an awesome undertaking (after all, you're talking about altering the very structure of the global Internet itself), but it really isn't that difficult. In practical terms, starting an alt. newsgroup is much easier than starting a newsgroup in one of the top-level hierarchies, but there are still a few tricks to it. Fortunately, as is the case with most questions one might have about how the Net works, there is a handy FAQ on the subject. To receive the FAQ, just send an e-mail message to **mail-server@rtfm.mit.edu**, with the following text in the body of the message:

send usenet/alt.config/So_You_Want_to_Create_ an_Alt_Newsgroup (be sure to include those funny-looking dashes between the words—use shift-hyphen on your keyboard). You will then receive by return e-mail a three-part FAQ that explains the process in detail. You can also read the FAQ on a Web page at **http:// www.math.psu.edu/barr/alt-creation-guide.html**.

Your first step in creating an alt. group should be to read the above FAQ, but just to whet your appetite (and to prove that it really isn't that difficult), here's a brief rundown of the process. Your next step is to post a proposal for your new group in the *alt.config* newsgroup (which is where news administrators, the folks who run the Usenet news servers at each site on the Net, hang out). Your proposal should be short and to the point, explaining why your group is necessary or desirable, why your subject isn't covered by existing groups, and so on. By the way, it's a good idea to read *alt.config* for at least a few weeks before you post your proposal, by which time you'll have a far better understanding of what to put in your proposal.

Once you've posted your proposal to *alt.config*, sit back and relax for a few weeks while comments on your idea roll in from other Net users. The real aim of this process is not to debate the virtues of Winthrop Fortescue as an author, but rather to demonstrate to the news administrators (who are looking over your shoulder, remember) that you're not a flake and that there is genuine public interest in your fledgling group. If public reaction to your idea in *alt.config* is generally positive, you're on your way.

Now it's time to ask the news administrator at your own site to issue the special "control message" to the Usenet network that will actually create your newsgroup. If for some reason you can't reach your own news administrator, you can always ask someone in *alt.config* itself to issue the control message. Once the control message is issued, the die is cast—either news administrators at other sites on the Net will decide to honor the control message and carry your group or they won't (and some may carry it while others may not). If you've come up with a good idea for a newsgroup and familiarized news administrators with your idea by way of a discussion in *alt.config*, the chances that your newsgroup will be carried by news servers around the world are quite good.

Don't be put off by the challenge of your undertaking; after all, someone recently created a newsgroup called **alt.cows.are.nice**, so it can't be that hard, can it? In the words of the FAQ, "There are no Guidelines or Rules for creating alt. groups. There is no one 'in charge' of the alt hierarchy. The key to creating a successful alt.newsgroup depends only on convincing the thousands of news administrators across the globe to carry your newsgroup." Piece of cake. After all, nobody doesn't like Winthrop Fortescue, right?

Chapter 5

MAILING LISTS: NEWS AND VIEWS IN YOUR E-MAILBOX

Of all the features of the Internet, probably the most versatile is e-mail, or electronic mail. The ability to send messages to another person thousands of miles away, almost instantaneously and without the need for stamps or a trip to the mailbox, is inarguably nifty. There have been many commentaries written on the social impact of the advent of e-mail—whether it sounds the death knell of "real" handwritten correspondence or whether the inherently ephemeral nature of e-mail means that it is taken less seriously than "hard copy" mail. One thing is certain: the ease of sending and receiving e-mail makes maintaining electronic correspondence so quick and painless that even newcomers to the Net often find themselves developing e-mail pen pals. Such relationships are not necessarily as ephemeral as the medium would lead some to believe;

stories abound of couples who have met, courted, and become engaged to be married, all via e-mail.

There are many ways to develop a group of e-mail pen pals—responding via e-mail directly to the author of a post in a Usenet newsgroup that you find insightful or clever, for instance, will usually garner at least a reply. There is even a Usenet newsgroup (*soc.penpals*) devoted entirely to matching likely Net pen pals, and a posting to that group stating one's interest ("book lover looking for same") is likely to produce a few candidates.

There is, however, an easier way to develop an e-mail correspondence with Net users who share your particular interest—often, in fact, with hundreds or thousands of like-minded people, all at one fell swoop. Joining an Internet mailing list will instantly make you a part of an on-line community of people who share your passion, whether it is gardening, ham radio, raising prizewinning gerbils or, of course, books and reading. As is the case with many aspects of the Net, exact figures are hard to come by, but there are more than 5,000 mailing lists operating on the Net and new ones spring up nearly every day.

Internet mailing lists were originally developed in the early days of the Net as a way for researchers to share results and participate in discussions with colleagues in their fields. Because participating in a mailing list requires only some sort of Net e-mail connection, it is possible to participate in a mailing list even if you lack any other sort of Internet access, such as Usenet or the Web.

Participating in a mailing list is simplicity incarnate. Once you join or subscribe to a given list, you will receive all e-mail messages sent to that list by other members. If you wish to make a contribution to the list, you simply send your e-mail message to the list address, and everyone else on the list will automatically receive your posting as an e-mail message.

The benefits of subscribing to a list are numerous. You'll be joining a community of people who share your specific interest, so your discussions will not be interrupted (as they often are on Usenet) by off-topic postings or annoying commercial advertisements. Because postings to the list come to you as e-mail messages, you'll have a complete, permanent record of what was said and not run the risk (as on Usenet) of missing part of a discussion if you don't tune in for a few days. You can always wait a day or two to open your e-mail, after all.

But perhaps the best aspect of participating in a mailing list is the remarkable sense of community that lists inspire. Because a mailing list is made up of people who have taken the time to join it (as opposed to merely wandering into a Usenet newsgroup by chance), list members often get to know each other fairly well, and the semi-private nature of the list encourages a more personal, trusting atmosphere than Usenet does. The sense of continuity encouraged by a list (many lists have lasted for more than 10 years) also lends both coherence and seriousness to discussions that you simply won't find on the open Net.

Because mailing lists were originally an academic invention, they offer particular attractions for users interested in books and reading. A mailing list devoted to Jane Austen, for instance, is likely to unite everyday fans of

Austen with serious academic students of her work. The discussions found on mailing lists devoted to literature often attain a depth of intellectual sophistication unknown on the rest of the Internet or, for that matter, in any other mass medium. At the same time, most lists manage to avoid a didactic tone, perhaps because participation is entirely voluntary, fueled by a genuine interest in the topic.

SUBSCRIBING TO A MAILING LIST

The key to every Net mailing list is the automatic software program called a "listserver" that runs the list, usually a program called "Listserv," "Listproc," or "Majordomo." The program runs on a central computer (often at a university) and receives all messages sent to the list and redistributes them to the other participants. Many listservers also archive, or keep a permanent transcript of, the contents of the list, and all listservers respond to commands that allow users to choose the form in which they receive the list (as separate messages or as a daily digest of messages).

Every mailing list has two addresses, and keeping the two straight is extremely important. One is the *listserver address*. This is the address of the central computer to which you send messages (called "user commands") to join the list, quit the list, or change your user options. The other address is the address of the list itself (the *list address*). This is where you should send messages that you want forwarded to the other subscribers of the list. *Never,*

never, send user commands to the list address. If you do, everyone who subscribes to the list will receive your commands and be very annoyed, but the listserver program itself will remain completely unaware of your wishes. There are few things more annoying to list participants than being deluged by repeated misdirected user commands from a clueless newcomer.

To join a list, send an e-mail message to the listserver address of the specific listserver. The message to join must be in a particular format, because it is being read by a computer, not a person. Leave the subject line of the message blank, and in the body of the message put subscribe *listname your personal name.* (If you're joining a Majordomo list, leave off your name entirely.) Be sure to use your personal name, not your e-mail address (the listserver will get your e-mail address from the header information on the message, so that's no problem). If you normally use a programmed signature on your e-mail messages, be sure to turn it off for this message, or you'll get an alarming error report from an irate listserver program by return e-mail.

There are a few (usually low-volume) lists that are run, not by listservers, but by actual human beings. In the case of these lists, just write directly to the list maintainer (called the "list owner") and ask to be added to the list.

FINDING A LIST TO JOIN

Although joining a list is a simple matter of sending an e-mail message to the listserver, finding a list you'd like to join is often a bit more difficult. As is the case with Usenet, there is no "Mailing List Central" running the show, and starting a list really only requires the cooperation of someone who owns a computer running a list-server program. Consequently, new lists appear frequently and there is no absolutely complete and reliable listing of what lists are available. On the other hand, there are a number of ways to find lists on a given subject.

The first step is to check Chapter 7 of this book, where you'll find many mailing lists indexed along with other Internet resources.

If you're interested in finding a list not included there, check the "Search the List of Lists" Web page at **http://catalog.com/vivian/interest-group-search.html**. This page searches the entire master list of mailing lists by any keyword you choose and will return a list of candidates, with a complete description of each list and subscription information. Vivian Neou, the creator of this page, is the current maintainer of the original "List of Lists" begun in the early days of the Internet by Rich Zellich. The entire "List of Lists" can also be retrieved via FTP from **ftp://ftp.nih.gov/network/interest.groups** or **ftp://sri.com/Netinfo/interest-groups.txt**, but keep in mind that this is a huge text file.

Another way to track down lists on a particular subject is to check an exhaustive compilation maintained by Stephanie De Silva called *Publicly Accessible Mailing Lists* (PAML). PAML is available several ways on the Net: it is periodically posted in a multipart format to the Usenet newsgroups **news.answers** and **news.announce. newusers**, and it is also available on Web pages at

**http://www.cis.ohio-state.edu/text/faq/usenet/mail/
mailing-lists/top.html** or **http://www.neosoft.com/
internet/paml**.

Another good source of list information is at **http://
www.tile.Net/tile/listserv**. The only drawback here is
that it includes only lists running on Listserv software
(and not Majordomo lists, for example). Yet another
source is Nova Southeastern University's E-Mail Discussion Group page at **http://www.nova.edu/Inter-Links/
listserv.html**. This page also offers help files containing
excellent background information on joining and working with mailing lists.

If you're looking for a list on an academic subject,
you'll probably want to check the *Directory of Scholarly
Electronic Conferences*, produced by Diane Kovacs and
the Directory Team at the Kent State University Libraries. The Directory is an exhaustive multipart catalog
of lists covering major subjects. It is available via e-mail
by sending the message "get acadlist.readme" to **list-
serv@kentvm.kent.edu**. You will receive return e-mail
listing available subject files, which you can then fetch via
e-mail with the appropriate "get" command.

Since there are new lists being created all the time,
you'll need a way to keep up with them. The easiest way
is to check the Usenet newsgroup *news.lists*, where announcements of new lists are posted. Another method is
to subscribe to the *Net Happenings* e-mail newsletter produced by Gleason Sackman, available by sending the
command "subscribe Net-happenings" (you don't need
to include your name) to **majordomo@dsmail.internic.
Net.** You'll receive daily listings, not just of new lists, but

of almost everything new on the Net as a whole. If you prefer to receive *Net Happenings* in digest form (which I highly recommend), just send the message "subscribe Net-happenings-digest" to the same address. Mr. Sackman's announcements are also posted to the Usenet newsgroup *comp.internet.net-happenings*.

There is also a mailing list dealing with announcements of new lists, available by sending the request "subscribe new-list" to **listserv@vm1.Nodak.Edu**.

Unless you're absolutely certain that you want to subscribe to a given list, it might be a good idea to ask for information about the list before you actually sign up. To do so, just send the message "info *listname your name*" to the list server instead of "subscribe *listname your name*." You'll then receive a file describing the list that will give you a better idea of what you're getting into.

Participating in a Mailing List

After you join a list, you'll probably begin receiving mail from the list within a day or two. You'll also receive an automatic confirmation message sent by the listserver, letting you know that your "subscribe" request was understood and that you are, in fact, now part of the list. *Save this message—it is extremely important.* It will tell you how to go about setting various list options, how to search the archives of the list if they exist, how to "pause" the list so you don't find 600 messages waiting when you get back from vacation, and how to quit the list. If you subscribe to more than one list, it's probably worth your time to create a special directory in your e-mail program for storing these messages. Even automated lists, by the way, have a human owner (listed in the confirmation message) whom you can contact in an emergency.

Remember that in joining a list you're actually joining an on-line community that may have existed for years before your arrival, so good manners require that you spend a bit of time reading the messages among list members before adding your two cents' worth. Once you've developed a feel for the group, go ahead and jump right in. In most cases, replying to a message from someone on the list is simply a matter of hitting the "reply" button in your e-mail program—the listserver program will automatically send copies of your message to everyone on the list. If you want to conduct a private correspondence with someone on the list, however, you'll have to make sure that you type their personal address, not the list address, into the "to" field of your reply. And, of course, if you ever decide to quit the list, you'll have to dig out that "welcome" message you received when you joined to find the proper address to which you should send your "quit" message.

MAILING LISTS AND YOUR SANITY

It may seem unlikely that, having found and joined a list devoted to your favorite subject, you would ever wish to leave it, but, trust me, there's a chance you will. Although Internet mailing lists are a wonderful invention, there are two main problems with many lists, and in some cases they become so severe that users bail out in frustration.

The first problem is volume. A busy list can generate hundreds of postings per week, and no matter how much you enjoy talking about the subject, there are still only 24 hours in a day and not enough time to read all of those messages. You may reach a point at which opening your e-mail program in the morning and finding 60 messages waiting to be read is simply too much to bear. Some lists give you the option of receiving the list in daily or weekly digest form, which may solve the problem for you (or make it easier to ignore, at least). Because of the volume generated by some lists, it's important to subscribe to lists one at a time, waiting for a week or so in order to gauge the traffic level of the new list before subscribing to another. Never subscribe to two or three lists on the same day. I've done it myself, and it's not a pretty sight when you start getting 200 messages every day.

The second problem with some lists is "topic drift": instead of talking about the avowed subject, participants drift into chatting about their children, their cats, or the movies they saw recently. You may find this sort of thing either charming or infuriating. Whether a given list drifts too far from its topic or not is a matter of taste, of course, but a good list will stick fairly close to the subject.

Chapter 6

How to Be Your Own Publisher: Putting Yourself On-line

A writer, someone once observed, is simply a reader moved by admiration to emulation. Just as there are few writers who are not also passionate readers, so there are few readers who have not at least dreamed of finding an audience for their creative endeavors. If you've ever yearned for a way to bring your poetry or prose to the public, your ship has arrived. The Internet is the largest self-publishing experiment in history. Think of it: the Internet "publishes" every day of the year; it is, for the most part, unedited and uncensored; and it has a global readership of between 30 million and 50 million people (at least a few hundred of whom are bound to recognize that poem you wrote to your cat as the masterpiece that it is). There are several ways to publish your own work or to find someone else to publish it on the Internet, all of which are open to anyone with a computer and Internet access. And, of course, there's always the chance that a major publisher will see your work on-line and offer you a huge contract and make your book an instant best-seller and pretty soon you'll be starring in a TV movie based on that poem you wrote to your cat. Hey, it's not impossible.

Posting Your Work on Usenet

Probably the easiest way to publish your own work on the Net is simply to post it to one of the Usenet newsgroups designed for just that purpose:

alt.prose   postings of original writings, both fiction and nonfiction

rec.arts.prose   short works of prose fiction and follow-up discussion

rec.arts.poems   for the posting of poems

There is also a newsgroup called **alt.prose.d**, where the "d" stands for "discussion," but a good deal of discussion takes place in **alt.prose** itself. It also is possible to post your writings in **alt.etext**, although that group tends to concentrate on electronic newsletters, "e-zines" (electronic magazines), and news of classic texts converted to digital form by groups such as Project Gutenberg.

The advantage of posting in one of these Usenet newsgroups is that you'll get instant exposure to a broad audience, and probably at least some public reaction to your work in the form of follow-up postings to your original message. The disadvantage of this method is that Usenet postings are by their very nature ephemeral, and your work will evaporate from most news servers within a few days. Publishing your work this way is a bit like writing it in chalk on the sidewalk: lots of people will see it if they happen to be passing by, but it will never end up in the Library of Congress. Still, it's a good way to start, and, assuming that public reaction to what you write is positive, it may give you just the encouragement you need to seek a higher-profile outlet for your work.

ELECTRONIC LITERARY JOURNALS AND E-ZINES

A way to see your work in print in a somewhat more prestigious (and more permanent) venue is to submit it to one of the hundreds of electronic journals and e-zines on the Internet. Going this route is not exactly self-publishing, since even the most informal e-zine has someone who acts as editor and chooses what to publish. But the good news is that, because there are so many new electronic publications on the Net (and more popping up every day), most on-line journals are actively seeking contributions from writers, so the chances of your work being accepted by one or more are actually quite good.

Most of the Net literary journals and e-zines listed in Chapter 7 accept submissions, and many of them post writers' guidelines on their home pages. Your first step should be to browse the ranks of on-line publications and pick a few that you are interested in submitting your work to; then contact the editors and briefly describe your work, asking how to submit it for consideration. Don't expect an immediate reply; many of the smaller e-zines are run by people with day jobs and busy lives. But don't worry—sooner or later you'll be able to tell your friends to check out your work at *http://www. bigtime.com.*

If you need further encouragement, keep in mind that some of these electronic journals are on-line outposts of respected print journals, so by being published on-line, you may be getting a foot in the door of the off-line publishing world.

Starting Your Own Electronic Newsletter

If you really feel that you have a lot to say that isn't being said elsewhere on the Internet, you may want to consider starting your own electronic newsletter. There are thousands of such newsletters on the Net, on just as many topics, delivering news and views on everything from mystery fiction (see The ClueLass Homepage at **http://www.slip.net/~cluelass/** for information) to miraculous encounters with angels (see **http://www. netangel.com/** for details), many with thousands of subscribers. If you'd like to get a sense of what's out there on the Net, just search at Yahoo (**http://www.yahoo.com**) under the word "newsletter"—the list you'll get goes on forever.

The secret of such newsletters' success is simplicity; a newsletter, after all, is just a glorified e-mail message sent to each subscriber. Each month, or week, or whatever, the newsletter's editor puts together a text file and mails it to the subscribers, just the way you'd send an e-mail message to your aunt.

E-mail newsletters can be modest or ambitious, but you're probably better off starting simple. Keep it short: less than 2,000 words is a good idea, especially because some e-mail programs that your subscribers may be using have difficulty accepting longer messages. Whether you plan to charge money for your newsletter is, of course, up to you, but keep in mind that the vast majority of Internet newsletters are free.

Once you have your newsletter ready to go, the next step is to announce it. The easiest way to do this is to post a brief announcement in the Usenet newsgroups to which your newsletter is most relevant. If your newsletter is about Scandinavian detective fiction, for instance, post your announcement to **rec.arts.mystery** as well as **rec.arts.books**. *Do not post the newsletter itself,* tempting as that may be. If you post the whole thing, you may inadvertently force anyone being charged by the minute for Internet access to pay to download your newsletter whether they're interested in it or not, which is hardly the way to win friends on the Net.

You should also announce your newsletter in the *Net Happenings* mailing list. The easiest way to do this is via the *Net Happenings* Web site (**http://www.mid.net:80/ net**), which features a handy submittal form you can fill out on the spot and explains exactly how to word your announcement.

Once your announcement is out on the Net, you'll start to get requests for your newsletter from people who want to subscribe. The important thing to do now is to save the return address from each of these messages—in most cases, that's where you'll be sending your newsletter. A good e-mail program, such as Eudora (available for both PCs and Macs), will allow you to extract the sender address from any mail you receive, but if you're using an on-line service's e-mail software, you may have to manually cut and paste the address into your e-mail address book. A good e-mail program will also allow you to create groups of addresses, which can make sending out your newsletter much simpler: just add new subscribers to a newsletter address group as they join, and when it's time to publish, send your newsletter to the entire group in one simple step. If your e-mail program won't allow you to create this kind of group, it may at least allow you to create separate folders within your address book, so at least subscribers' addresses won't get mixed in with those of anyone else you happen to have.

Mailing your newsletter yourself is the best way to start out, but once your creation becomes popular (more than 100 subscribers or so), you'll probably find that dealing with subscription requests and mailing hundreds of copies of your newsletter becomes unmanageable. When you reach this point, you may want to look into converting your newsletter to a mailing list newsletter running on a Listserv or Majordomo computer program, which will manage the day-to-day details (see Chapter 5 for an explanation of how these programs work). Since most of these listserver programs are run on large computers at universities and other institutions, you'll probably have to find someone willing to give you space on their listserver. Your first step in finding such space is the logical one: ask your subscribers. There's a good chance they'll know someone who can help. You can also post a query in the Usenet newsgroups where you first announced your newsletter. This should do the trick, but if all else fails, drop a note to the editor of a similar newsletter that is distributed as a mailing list (another mystery newsletter, for example), and you're almost certain to get good advice.

PUBLISHING YOURSELF ON THE WORLD WIDE WEB

Judging by the recent explosion in the number of aspiring writers' and poets' home pages on the World Wide Web, a great untapped reservoir of creative energy has finally found its outlet. Personal Web pages, stored in individual users' home directories on Web servers maintained by access providers, now number in the tens of thousands. They range from simple "here I am and here's a picture of my cat" pages to some of the most valuable and entertaining sites on the Web. Many of the resources listed in this book, in fact, began as personal home pages and now receive thousands of "hits," or visitors, every day.

If you've always dreamed of finding a place to publish your own writing, you've probably realized by now that a personal Web page might just be the answer to your prayers, an easy way to bring your work directly to a worldwide audience numbering in the tens of millions.

What can you put on your Web page? Anything your heart desires—poems or essays, favorite cookie recipes, that novel you started to write in college, the story of your family. If it's yours and it's legal, you can put it on the Web page. You can't include someone else's copyrighted material, however, but you're free to add links to any other resource on the Net. If you think The Shakespeare Web (**http://www.shakespeare.com**), for example, is especially neat, you can put a link on your page that will take your visitors directly there with just a mouse click.

What's Behind That Web Page?

Looking at some of the visually striking personal pages on the Web, you'd never guess the big secret about Web sites, which is that creating one really isn't that hard. In fact, it's remarkably simple (honest!) and if you have a word processing program, some sort of Internet connection, and a basic familiarity with saving and moving files, you're already halfway there.

Every Web page you see on your screen is actually a document, a file similar to one you might work with in a word processing program. But instead of being a WordPerfect or Microsoft Word file, Web pages are in the HTML (hypertext markup language) format. The HTML document itself is in the standard ASCII (plain text) format. What makes it an HTML document is that it is full of what are called "HTML tags," which are formatting codes—simply directions for the browser to follow in displaying the page.

Let's suppose that I'm typing a memo in WordPerfect, and I want a certain paragraph to appear in boldface. I highlight the text and click on "bold," thereby inserting "begin bold" and "end bold" codes at either end of the paragraph, right? Well, if I'm making a Web page and want a paragraph to be in boldface, I just insert a tag that says "<bold>" at the beginning and one that says "<bold>" at the end. That's it—I told you it was simple. As a matter of fact, the folks who invented HTML had to keep it simple, because HTML had to be able to work on any sort of computer, not just one system.

There are many more codes than just "<bold>" in HTML, of course, but the principle for all of them is the same. There are simple codes for headline styles, slightly more complicated codes for inserting pictures onto the page, codes for links to other pages, and even new codes that only certain browsers (mostly notably Netscape) can interpret. But all of them are ultimately straightforward and logical.

Learning HTML

The best way to learn HTML and all the other things you'll need to know in order to create a "killer home page" is to read one of the many books available on the subject. Two titles I'd recommend are:

Teach Yourself Web Publishing With HTML 3.0 In A Week (Laura Lemay, Sams Publishing Co., 1996, $29.95) A very lucid and logical tutorial. And it works—I learned HTML from a previous edition.

The Web Page Design Cookbook (William Horton, et al., John Wiley & Sons, 1996, $34.95) A well-done explanation of HTML that includes a CD-ROM with templates of Web pages you can use to create your own site.

If you'd like to take a peek at how some of your favorite Web pages were developed, just click on the "View Source" or "View HTML" menu item in your Web browser next time you're on-line, and you'll see the coding. You usually can save the coded text to your own hard drive to study later, which is a great way to pick up HTML coding tricks.

Web Page Construction Tools

It's possible to create a Web page using nothing more than a simple word processing program (as long as it can save documents in ASCII text, which most programs can), but the truth is that typing all those little tags gets very tiresome very quickly. Users of the Microsoft Word and WordPerfect word processing systems have a head start: current versions of those programs have been upgraded to incorporate HTML editing functions, allowing users to create HTML documents easily.

If you don't use one of those word processing systems, there are several free or nearly free HTML authoring tools available. These programs are basically text editors (they do all their work in ASCII to begin with) with buttons you can click on to insert all the codes you'll ever want to use. The best place to find these programs is on the Net itself—check out the Jumbo Shareware Archives at **http://www.**

jumbo.com, or simply search Yahoo at **http://www. yahoo.com** using the search term "HTML editor."

If you're using one of the major on-line services and you're interested in creating a fairly simple Web page, you're in luck. Each of these services offers the ability to create a personal home page and, even better, an automatic program that you can download from the service itself to handle the process for you. The program will lead you through a question-and-answer session to determine just how you want the page to look ("Picture of cat—yes or no?"), then do all the coding and upload the page to the service for you.

Finally, if you don't use one of the major on-line services but you're eager to develop a Web page without learning any HTML at all, there's a free program available that's similar to the automatic programs offered by the on-line services. Called *Web Wizard*, the program will lead you through a simple question-and-answer session and give you a completed, albeit rudimentary, personal Web page when it's done. *Web Wizard* is available at **http://www.halcyon.com/artamedia/webwizard/**.

Once you've completed your Web page, it's a good idea to test it by looking at it with a Web browser while the page is still on the hard drive of your home computer; it's much easier to fix any glitches at this stage than after the page is up and running on the Web. Most browsers will allow you to open and view a local file on your hard drive (look in the "File" menu of your browser), although you may have to sign onto your Internet access provider, open the browser, then sign off to get the browser running. Once you have your page displayed in the browser, be sure to carefully proofread the text. Nothing will turn off visitors to your page more than careless typographical errors. If you've included links to other places on the Web, sign on to your access provider, load your page from the hard drive, and click on those links to make sure that they actually work and will take your visitors where you want them to go.

Putting Your Page On-line

Once your page is done and checked, your last hurdle is to get it up and running on the Web. This usually isn't difficult, but how you do it will depend on how you access the Net. Most Internet service providers will provide free space on their servers to store pages. They also have developed painless ways for customers to upload and maintain personal Web pages, so all you need to do is ask the customer support folks at your service. You'll probably need to use an FTP program (see Chapter 3) to transfer the files into your home directory. I do it myself every two weeks when I update my home page, and the whole process takes me less than 10 minutes each time.

If you're using a major on-line service, you're in luck again: its Web page creation program will guide you through the steps necessary to upload your page on the service's Web server.

Points to Ponder About Your Web Page

There are a few pitfalls to avoid in designing a Web page. Don't overload it with large or fancy graphics—they take forever to download on a slow link and will only annoy your visitors. The same goes for fancy fonts and background images: simple is always better on the Web. Take the time to find out how to make your page visible to visitors using any sort of browser, not just the latest generation of Netscape. Ideally, visitors should have a reason to come visit your page even if they're using a text-only browser such as Lynx and can't see your pretty pictures and fancy design.

That last consideration brings us back to the question of content and the Web. The only reason for people to come back again and again to your page is the content you put there. If you build it, they will come once, but they'll only come back if there's something interesting. Give folks something to read, on the other hand, and update it often, and you'll be a hit. So much of the Web is a wasteland of computer gimmickry, "cyberpunk" juvenalia, and bad jokes that anything actually readable will win fans in droves.

This means that there is a ready-made audience, potentially in the thousands, for almost anything you've written. For example, I post my thrice-weekly newspaper column to my Web page (somewhat after it has run in the newspapers that pay for it, of course), and I've gradually built up an audience of more than a thousand regular visitors (it's at **http://www.interport.net/~words1**, since you asked). Best of all, I've discovered that if I'm late in updating my page, I actually get irate e-mail from readers demanding to know where the new columns are. This is enormously gratifying, and although my humble page will never attain the status of the Time-Warner or CNN sites, it's nice to know that reading what I write has become part of quite a few folks' weekly routine.

So dust off that old play, or poem, or screenplay, or book review, or write something brand new, and put it up there on the Web where it belongs.

Chapter 7

❖

ON-LINE RESOURCES FOR BOOK LOVERS

Compiling a catalog of the Internet, even one focusing on a single topic, is a daunting task. The culprit is the constant, explosive growth of the Internet itself. Like a boisterous child, the Net will simply not sit still to have its picture taken. While the World Wide Web, for example, consisted of just a few hundred sites in late 1993, as of early 1996 there were well over 100,000 Web sites, each of which may house hundreds of pages. Alta Vista (**http://www. altavista.digital.com**), one of the newer Net search engines, boasts an index of more than 16 million individual Web pages. Anyone attempting to round up everything available on the Internet will quickly learn just how frazzled the sorcerer's apprentice felt.

In compiling this list of Internet resources, I've focused on Net sites that bring a variety of reading resources together in one place, are themselves especially interesting or unusual, or are representative of a particular type of resource. Rather than including the location of every single on-line bookstore or e-text on the Internet, for example, I've listed a few samples and highlighted on-line directories where many more can be found.

Most of the resources noted here are available to anyone with access to the Internet, but I've also included a representative sampling of resources available only through one or another of the large commercial on-line services (CompuServe, Prodigy, and America Online) because many readers will be accessing the Internet through one of those services. I've also included a sampling of the more than 250 conferences (discussion groups) available through The WELL, a smaller on-line service of special interest to readers (see Chapter 2). Resources available only to users of a particular on-line service are preceded in this list by the name of the service in boldface.

The list is arranged roughly by genre—romance, mystery, science fiction, and so on—as well as by a few other logical categories. Although I've included Gopher, FTP, and telnet resources, the list is very heavily weighted in favor of World Wide Web sites, as the Web is the most popular, the most easily accessible, and arguably the most innovative part of today's Internet. The Web also offers the enormous advantage of interconnectivity: nearly every Web site listed here contains links to dozens, sometimes hundreds, of other Web pages of interest to the book lover. This list, therefore, should be viewed as a collection of starting points, not destinations.

Within many sections of this list you will find Usenet

discussion groups and mailing lists related to literature as well as to the particular topic of each section. Many more newsgroups and mailing lists focusing on some of these interest areas (science fiction, for instance) exist than I have included here, but I've chosen the mailing lists and newsgroups specifically dealing with the literature of that particular subject. If you're interested in finding other Usenet newsgroups, visit the Liszt of Newsgroups Web page (**http://www.liszt.com/**), where you'll be able to search for newsgroups by topic. Similarly, a search of the Publicly Accessible Mailing Lists Web page (**http://www.neosoft.com/internet/paml/**) will direct you to other mailing lists devoted to your area of interest.

Detailed instructions for subscribing to mailing lists can be found in Chapter 5. In this chapter, the name or subject of the list is given first, followed by the formal name (what you should call it when sending a subscription or other request to the automatic listserver program that runs the list), then the address of the listserver carrying the list. In almost every case, subscribing is simply a matter of sending an e-mail message to the listserver address (which I have helpfully identified by **Mail to:** in each mailing list entry), leaving the subject line blank and the body of the message reading **subscribe listname your name** (e.g., **subscribe DOROTHY-L Bob Bookworm**). If the list address is a Majordomo program (e.g., **majordomo@bowwow.edu**), it's not necessary to include your name in the message.

Equally important information about participating in Usenet newsgroups can be found in Chapter 4.

Every effort has been made to ensure that the addresses

of the resources listed here are accurate, but if you should discover that something has become inaccessible or has changed its address, please drop me a note at **words1@ interport.net**, so that it can be corrected in future editions of this book. Similarly, if you feel that I have inexplicably overlooked a great literary site on the Net, please let me know.

Note: Comments on a particular site contained within quotation marks are taken from the site's own description of itself. All other comments are the author's personal opinions. Your mileage may vary.

UNDERSTANDING NAMES AND PLACES ON THE INTERNET

The Internet is a very big place, made up of thousands of computers located all over the world. Because no one really "runs" the Internet, there is no map an explorer can depend on, and no "Directory Assistance" to call for help in finding a particular person or place on the Net. Fortunately, there are several ways to search the Internet, as well as detailed directories by the score.

Every computer on the Internet has a unique address, which (once you find out what it is) makes connecting to computers on the other side of the world as easy as dialing a phone number. In this book I have used the standard format for Internet addresses, known as the uniform resource locator, or URL. Each URL consists of a string of letters or numbers, for example, **http://www. interport.net/~words1**.

In each URL, the letters preceding the colon denote the method used to access the site:

> **http:** or hypertext transfer protocol: a site on the World Wide Web
> **ftp:** or file transfer protocol: a file that can be downloaded to your home computer
> **telnet:** a telnet computer that you can log onto
> **gopher:** a Gopher server for accessing remote file libraries

All of these access methods are explained in Chapter 3.

The letters and numbers after the colon, which are always preceded by a double forward slash, identify the specific computer or site to which you'll be connecting. In the example above, **http** identifies the resource as a site on the World Wide Web, **www.interport.net** identifies the specific host computer, and **/~words1** identifies the specific directory on that computer's hard drive in which the resource resides. (I should probably note at this point that the example I'm using is my own home page on the Web.) The odd character before "**words1**" in the last part of the address is a tilde (found in the upper left-hand section of most keyboards), which is often used to denote a particular individual's home directory on a computer that may have thousands of users. Occasionally you'll see a URL that includes scored spaces (e.g., **ftp://ftp.neato.com/stuff/neat_stuff.txt**)—just be sure to use the shifted character on the same key with the hyphen.

All the resources mentioned in this book are identified

in the standard URL format, in the form **http://
www.interport.net/~wordsl**.

In many cases, you won't need to type in the entire
URL. In other words, if you're connecting to an FTP
site, you won't have to type **http:ftp://ftp.rtfm.mit.edu**"—
just **ftp.rtfm.mit.edu**.

Certain Web browsers do require you to type in the
full URL, beginning with **http:**, in order to tell the
browser the type of site to which it's connecting. Other
browsers, most notably Netscape, can determine this information automatically, but when in doubt, it doesn't
hurt to type the entire address.

If You Have Problems With an Internet Address

Because Internet addresses can be complex, typographical errors in both print and on-line directories are not
uncommon. It's also not uncommon for resources on
the Net to change their addresses. Sometimes you'll call
up a Web page and find a forwarding address, but many
times you'll get the dreaded message "Error 404—that
file does not exist on this server." [One e-zine on the
Web has even waggishly taken "Error 404" as its title
(**http://www.cban.com/error404/**).] If you're trying to
access a particular site and repeatedly receive only error
messages for your efforts, you may be able to reach
your goal by cropping the address. If **ftp.neato.com/
stuff/neat_stuff.txt** doesn't work, try **ftp.neato.
com/stuff/**. This method, when it works, will connect
you to the parent directory of the directory or file you
were looking for in the first place. From there, you can

find the file you want by simply looking through the parent directory. The name of the file may be slightly different from what you had been told, or it may have been moved to a different directory, but if it exists at the site, you'll probably find it with a little poking around.

INTERNET METAPAGES, INDEXES, AND SEARCH ENGINES

While the Internet as a whole is notoriously unorganized, with its best resources often scattered literally all over the globe, finding things on the Net is often quite simple with the aid of the numerous indexes, lists, and search engines available on the Net itself.

General Indexes and Metapages

The following is a selected list of general resource indexes of the Internet. (A metapage is essentially a list of lists.) These sources are probably your best starting points when searching for information on any particular subject. They also make for fascinating browsing even if you're not looking for anything in particular.

Clearinghouse for Subject-Oriented Internet Resource Guides No matter what you're looking for on the Net, someone has probably written a guide on how to find it. This is a list of all of those helpful guides.
http://www.lib.umich.edu/chhome.html

<u>Daedalus's Guides to the Web: Net and Web Resources and Information</u> A great page with links to many lists of Net resources.
http://www.georgetown.edu/labyrinth/general/ general.html

<u>Meta-Index of WWW Resources, Library of Congress</u> A bird's-eye view of resources available on the Web.
http://lcweb.loc.gov/global/metaindex.html

<u>Meta-Index of WWW and Internet Resources (NCSA)</u> A general index of the Net.
http://www.ncsa.uiuc.edu/SDG/Software/Mosaic/Meta Index.html

<u>New Riders' Official World Wide Web Yellow Pages</u> The Web version of a popular reference book. Search by keyword or subject.
http://www.mcp.com/nrp/wwwyp/

<u>The Whole Internet Catalog (GNN Select)</u> A classic (and very good) index.
http://gnn.com/wic/wics/index.html

<u>Yahoo</u> It's not just a search engine—it's also probably the best overall index of the Internet, and features a lucid branching-tree directory structure.
http://www.yahoo.com

Search Engines

Don't let the term "search engine" scare you—all you need to do is type in the subject you're interested in, click on a button, and sit back while these cyber-bloodhounds sniff out the goodies. Each search engine has its own particular strengths and weaknesses, so if at first you don't succeed in finding what you're looking for, try another one. As a matter of fact, try another one even if you think you've succeeded the first time, because there's always more of everything out there on the Net.

All-in-One Search Page A handy site that offers access to all the major search engines on one Web page. Also offers software and e-mail address searching.
http://www.albany.net/allinone/

Altavista A very powerful search engine based on a full-text index of more than 16 million Web pages.
http://www.altavista.digital.com

Excite Netsearch Also offers reviews of many Web sites.
http://www.excite.com/

InfoSeek Home Page Offers both free Web searches and fee-based searches of commercial databases.
http://www.infoseek.com/Home

Inktomi Search Engine A recent entry in the Web searching race; very fast.
http://inktomi.berkeley.edu/query.html

Lycos Home Page Another very powerful search engine.
http://www.lycos.com/

Magellan Offers minireviews of the sites it finds for you.
http://www.mckinley.com/

SavvySearch Sends your query to 15 separate search engines, then displays the results in a single list.
http://www.cs.colostate.edu/~dreiling/smartform.html

<u>WebCrawler Searching</u> Good for simple searches; usually very fast.
http://webcrawler.com/

<u>Yahoo</u> One of the first, and still one of the best, Web search engines. Yahoo also incorporates an excellent browsable index of Web resources.
http://www.yahoo.com

Indexes of Resources for Book Lovers

The indexes listed here include books on-line, bookstores, pointers to literary discussion groups, general literary resources, and links to other, more specialized, indexes. Many of these indexes and lists, in true hypertext fashion, refer to each other, so any one index will probably lead you eventually to anything found in any other index.

<u>American Studies Web: Literature and Hypertext</u> A list of sites mostly relating to American literature. Includes links to pages devoted to individual authors.
http://pantheon.cis.yale.edu/~davidp/lit.html

<u>Arthurian Home Page</u> As in King Arthur.
http://calvin.stemnet.nf.ca/~djohnsto/arthur.html

<u>Arts and Humanities via Gopher</u> A Web page featuring an extensive list of literature available by Gopher.
http://galaxy.einet.net/GJ/arts.html

<u>Book Lovers: Fine Books and Literature</u> A great resource page for book lovers, frequently updated and worth visit-

ing on a regular basis. The author of the page keeps a sharp eye out for new resources on the Net.
http://www.xs4all.nl/~pwessel/

Book Stacks—Electronic Library Features a wide variety of public domain texts.
http://www.books.com/scripts/lib.exe

BookWeb The American Booksellers Association home page. It offers information on publishers, media, etc., as well as an overview of on-line resources.
http://ambook.org/bookweb/

BookWire "The First Place to Look for Book Information"—another great site with links to almost everywhere.
http://www.bookwire.com/

Canadian Literature Archive From the University of Manitoba.
http://canlit.st-john.umanitoba.ca/Canlitx/ Canlit_homepage.html

Classics Guide A guide to classical resources on-line.
http://nervm.nerdc.ufl.edu/~blaland/classics.html

The English Server A great site with fascinating content as well as neatly organized links to resources on anything connected to English literature.
http://english-server.hss.cmu.edu/

Frequently Asked Questions (FAQ) About Book Newsgroups Where to find information on a variety of sub-

jects among the many Usenet newsgroups devoted to books and reading.
http://www.cis.ohio-state.edu:80/hypertext/faq/ usenet/books/top.html

Internet Book Information Center Maintains the World Wide Web Virtual Library on Literature, which contains hundreds of links to literary sites on the Net.
http://sunsite.unc.edu/ibic/IBIC-homepage.html

Internet Public Library (IPL) A genuine on-line library, with a reference desk and tons of resources.
http://ipl.sils.umich.edu/

Labyrinth Home Page A well-organized overview of medieval literature on-line.
http://www.georgetown.edu/labyrinth/ labyrinth-home.html

Literature on the Internet A hypertext version of the comprehensive FAQ file compiled by Dr. Wolfgang Hink.
http://www.cis.ohio-state.edu:80/text/faq/usenet/ internet/literaryresources/faq.html

Literature at Yahoo The folks at Yahoo do a great job of cataloging literary resources on the Web. They label the new ones, so check here frequently.
http://www.yahoo.com/Arts/Humanities/Literature/

LitLinks, University of Alberta Links to a wide variety of literary resources.
http://www.ualberta.ca/~englishd/litlinks.htm

LitWeb A well-organized overview of readers' and writers' resources.
http://www.vmedia.com/shannon/litweb.html

Mimi Why "Mimi"? Who knows? The menu lists resources pertaining to American authors through the late 19th century.
http://www.keele.ac.uk/depts/as/Literature/amlit. mimi.html

Online Book Initiative An eclectic selection of e-texts available via Gopher.
gopher://gopher.std.com/ll/obi/book

On-line Books Page An index developed at Carnegie-Mellon University of over 1,000 on-line books.
http://www.cs.cmu.edu/Web/books.html

OZ Lit An index of Australian literature on-line.
http://www.vicnet.net.au/~ozlit/index.html

Planet Earth Home Page A directory of on-line books and libraries.
http://www.nosc.mil/planet_earth/books.html

Project Gutenberg Master Index The master list of all books converted to e-text by Project Gutenberg. The goal of the project is to make 10,000 texts available on-line by the year 2000.
http://jg.cso.uiuc.edu/pg/welcome.html
or
http://www.w3org/hypertext/DataSources/ bySubject/Literature/Gutenberg/Overview.html

Usenet newsgroup: **bit.listserv-gutnberg-1**

Project Runeberg Scandinavian books and culture.
http://www.lysator.liu.se/runeberg/

Rare Books Around the Net Links for bibliophiles.
http://www.abaa-booknet.com/discuss.html

Rec.arts.books FAQ A 14-part FAQ file for the primary
Usenet newsgroup for book lovers.
**http://www.cis.ohio-state.edu:80/hypertext/faq/
usenet/books/faq/faq.html**

Sally Anne Picks up where Mimi (see separate entry)
leaves off; a repository of 20th-century American
literature.
**http://www.keele.ac.uk/depts/as/Literature/amlit.
sallyanne.html**

UNCAT: The Catalog of the Uncataloged Books,
newsletters, and more that never made it into *Books in
Print.*
http://www.sapphire.com/uncat

Victorian Web Overview Late-19th-century literary resources on the Web.
**http://www.stg.brown.edu/projects/hypertext/landow
/victorian/victov.html**

VoS English Literature *Voice of the Shuttle* English literature page—covers a broad range of literary genres and
periods.
http://humanitas.ucsb.edu/shuttle/english.html

The Wiretap Electronic Text Archive Large collections
of e-texts available via Gopher.
gopher://wiretap.spies.com

<u>The Word</u> An eclectic list that includes e-zines, on-line books, related resources, and unusual links.
http://www.speakeasy.org/~dbrick/Hot/word.html

<u>The Write Page</u> An excellent collection of resources, arranged by genre.
http://www.writepage.com/

USENET NEWSGROUPS

  alt.appalachian.literature
  alt.books.beatgeneration
  alt.books.technical
  bit.listserv-literary
  rec.arts.books
  sci.classics

Frequently Asked Questions (FAQ) Files

The following list is drawn with permission from Dr. Wolfgang Hink's excellent *Guide to Literature on the Internet*, which includes FAQ and other informational files pertaining to reading and literature. The current version of Dr. Hink's guide is available by e-mail by sending a message to **mail-server@rtfm.mit.edu**. The body of the message should read "**send usenet/news. answers/Internet/literary-resources**" (leave the subject line blank). It can also be retrieved via FTP at **ftp://rtfm. mit.edu/pub/usenet/news.answers/Internet/literary-resources**, or at **http://www.cis.ohio-state.edu:80/text/ faq/usenet/Internet/literary-resources/faq.html.**

Many of these FAQs are posted periodically in the relevant newsgroups (noted in the "Newsgroups" line of each item), as well as in the *news.answers* newsgroup. Most are also available from the **rtfm.mit.edu** archive via FTP at **ftp://ftp.rtfm.mit.edu/pub/usenet/news.answers/[archive name]**. (The archive is given for each entry.) You can also obtain the FAQs by sending an e-mail message to **mailserver@rtfm.mit.edu**. The body of the message should read **send usenet/news.answers/[archive-name]** (leave the subject line blank).

If there is no archive name listed, wait to see if the FAQ appears in the relevant newsgroup or in the **news.answers** newsgroup, or request the FAQ from the author directly, at the e-mail address noted in each entry.

alt.books.reviews FAQ
    Newsgroups: alt.books.reviews, rec.arts.books,
        rec.answers, alt.answers, news.answers
    From: sbrock@teal.csn.org (Steve Brock)
    Archive name: books/reviews-faq

alt.comics.alternative FAQ
    Newsgroups: alt.comics.alternative
    From: kap1@wimpy.cpe.uchicago.edu (Dietrich J. Kappe)

alt.cyberpunk FAQ
    Newsgroups: alt.cyberpunk, alt.answers, news.answers
    From: erich@hrl8.cs.tamu.edu (Erich Schneider)
    Archive name: cyberpunk-faq

alt.fan.douglas-adams FAQ
    Newsgroups: alt.fan.douglas-adams, alt.answers,
      news. answers
    From: nhughes@tiamat.umd.umich.edu (Nathan
      Hughes)
    Archive name: douglas-adams-FAQ

alt.fan.dune FAQ
    Newsgroups: alt.fan.dune, alt.answers,
      news.answers
    From: cgilmore@phoenix.princeton.edu
    Archive name: sf/dune-faq

alt.fan.pern FAQ
    Newsgroups: alt.fan.pern, news.answers,
      alt.answers
    From: quirk@unm.edu (Taki Kogoma)
    Archive name: pern-intro/part1 [-2]

alt.fan.piers-anthony FAQ
    Newsgroups: alt.fan.piers-anthony, alt.answers,
      news.answers
    From: umholme0@cc.UManitoba.CA (Douglas
      Holmes)
    Archive name: books/piers-anthony-faq

alt.fan.pratchett FAQ
    Newsgroups: alt.fan.pratchett, news.answers,
      alt.answers
    From: gnat@kauri.vuw.ac.nz (Nathan Torkington)
    Archive name: pratchett/faq

alt.fan-pratchett Mini-FAQ
  Newsgroups: alt.fan.pratchett
  From: leo@cp.tn.tudelft.nl (Leo Breebaart)
  Archive name: pratchett-mini-faq

alt.folklore.ghost-stories FAQ
  Newsgroups: alt.folklore.ghost-stories, alt.paranormal,
    alt.paranet.paranormal, alt.answers, news.answers
  From: obiwan@Netcom.com (obiwan)
  Archive name: folklore/ghost-stories

alt.history.what-if FAQ
  Newsgroups: alt.history.what-if, alt.answers,
    news.answers
  From: altworld@panix.com (Robert B. Schmunk)
  Archive name: history/what-if

alt.quotations FAQ
  Newsgroups: alt.quotations, alt.answers, news.answers
  From: dok@fwi.uva.nl
  Archive name: quotations/part1

alt.sex.stories FAQ
  Newsgroups: alt.sex.stories, alt.sex.stories.d
  From: laff@headop.cs.uiuc.edu (Joshua A. Laff)

alt.usage.english FAQ
  Newsgroups: alt.usage.english, alt.answers,
    news.answers
  From: misrael@csi.uottawa.ca (Mark Israel)
  Archive name: alt-usage-english-faq

Alternate History Stories
    Newsgroups: rec.arts.sf.written, alt.history.what-if,
        rec.answers, alt.answers, news.answers
    From: altworld@panix.com (Robert B. Schmunk)
    Archive name: sf/alt_history/part1 [-8]

Arthurian Booklist
    Newsgroups: rec.arts.books, rec.answers,
        news.answers
    From: tittle@Netcom.com (Cindy Tittle Moore)
    Archive name: books/arthurian

Isaac Asimov FAQ
    Newsgroups: alt.books.isaac-asimov, alt.answers,
        news. answers
    From: John_Jenkins@taligent.com (John H.
        Jenkins)
    Archive name: books/isaac-asimov-faq/part1 [-2]

Basement Full of Books
    Newsgroups: rec.arts.books, rec.answers,
        news.answers
    From:mcintyre@cpac.washington.edu (Vonda N.
        McIntyre)
    Archive name: books/basement-full-of-books

Book Catalogues and Book Clubs List (rec.arts.books)
    Newsgroups: rec.arts.books, rec.answers,
        news.answers
    From: tittle@Netcom.com (Cindy Tittle Moore)
    Archive name: books/catalogues

Books by Mail (FAQ)
  Newsgroups: rec.arts.books, rec.arts.sf.written,
    rec.answers, news.answers
  From: ecl@mtgp003.mt.att.com (Evelyn C. Leeper)
  Archive name: books/ship-by-mail

Bookstores in Eastern North American Cities (FAQ)
  Newsgroups: rec.arts.books, rec.arts.sf.written,
    rec.answers, news.answers
  From: ecl@mtgp003.mt.att.com (Evelyn C. Leeper)
  Archive name: books/stores/north-american/
    eastern

Bookstores in New York City (NYC) List (FAQ)
  Newsgroups: rec.arts.books, rec.arts.sf.written,
    ny.general, nyc.general, nj.general, rec.answers,
    news.answers
  From: ecl@mtgp003.mt.att.com (Evelyn C. Leeper)
  Archive name: books/stores/north-american/nyc

Bookstores in Northern North American Cities (FAQ)
  Newsgroups: rec.arts.books, rec.arts.sf.written,
    rec.answers, news.answers
  From: ecl@mtgp003.mt.att.com (Evelyn C. Leeper)
  Archive name: books/stores/north-american/
    northern

Bookstores in San Diego
  Newsgroups: rec.arts.books, rec.arts.books.childrens,
    la.forsale, relcom.fido.su.books
  From: jamesd@cg57.esNet.com (James Davis)

Bookstores in San Francisco Bay Area (SF) List (FAQ)
   Newsgroups: rec.arts.books, rec.arts.sf.written,
      ba.general, rec.answers, news.answers
   From: ecl@mtgp003.mt.att.com (Evelyn C. Leeper)
   Archive name: books/stores/north-american/bay-area

Bookstores in Various Asian Cities List (FAQ)
   Newsgroups: rec.arts.books, rec.arts.sf.written,
      rec.answers, news.answers
   From: ecl@mtgp003.mt.att.com (Evelyn C. Leeper)
   Archive name: books/stores/asian

Books in Various European Cities List (FAQ)
   Newsgroups: rec.arts.books, rec.arts.sf.written,
      rec.answers, news.answers
   From: ecl@mtgp003.mt.att.com (Evelyn C. Leeper)
   Archive name: books/stores/european

Bookstores in Western North American Cities (FAQ)
   Newsgroups: rec.arts.books, rec.arts.sf.written,
      rec.answers, news.answers
   From: ecl@mtgp003.mt.att.com (Evelyn C. Leeper)
   Archive name: books/stores/north-american/
      western

Classical Studies FAQ
   Newsgroups: sci.classics, sci.answers,
      news.answers
   From: jamie@akeake. its.vuw.ac.nz (Jamieson
      Norrish)
   Archive name: classics-faq

Classics FTP, Gopher, WWW, etc., Sites
   Newsgroups: sci.classics
   From: jsruebel@iastate.edu (James S. Ruebel)

Grading Guide (To Preserve and Protect Comics)
   Newsgroups: rec.arts.comics.info,
      rec.arts.comics.misc
   From: paul@erc.msstate.edu (Paul Adams)

Grading Guide (Grading Comics)
   Newsgroups: rec.arts.comics.info,
      rec.arts.comics.marketplace
   From: paul@ERC.MsState.Edu (Paul Adams)

Internet Mall: Shopping the Information Highway
   Newsgroups: alt.internet.services, comp.newprod,
      alt.answers, comp.answers, news.answers
   From: taylor@Netcom.com (Dave Taylor)
   Archive name: Internet-services/Internet-mall

Internet Top 100 SF List FAQ
   Newsgroups: rec.arts.books
   From: tcooke@maths.adelaide.edu.au (Tristrom
   Cooke)

Internet Writer Resource Guide
   Newsgroups: misc.writing, rec.arts.prose, rec.arts.sf.
      written, misc.answers, rec.answers, news.answers
   From: t.lawrence@auntie.bbcnc.org.uk (Trevor
   Lawrence)
   Archive name: writing/resources

Journalism Resources on the Internet
   Newsgroups: alt.journalism, alt.politics.media,
      alt.news-media, alt.answers, news.answers
   From: verbwork@access.digexNet (John S. Makulowich)
   Archive name: journalism-Net-resources

James Joyce FAQ
   Newsgroups: rec.arts.books
   From: jorn@MCS.COM (Jorn Barger)

Media List
   Newsgroups: alt.journalism, alt.internet.services
   From: adamg@world.std.com (Adam M. Gaffin)

misc.books.technical FAQ
   Newsgroups: misc.books.technical, misc.answers,
      news.answers
   From: rathinam@worf.infonet.net (Sethu R. Rathinam)
   Archive name: books/technical

misc.writing FAQ
   Newsgroups: misc.writing, news.answers,
      misc.answers
   From: lsefton@apple.com
   Archive name: writing/FAQ

misc.writing FAQ: Recommended Reading
   Newsgroups: misc.writing, misc.answers,
      news.answers
   From: lsefton@apple.com
   Archive name: writing/bibliography

Murder Mysteries Set in Ancient Rome (Booklist)
   Newsgroups: rec.arts.mystery, sci.classics,
      alt.books.reviews
   From: heli@netcom.com (Rick Heli)

Nautical Fiction List [2 parts]
   Newsgroups: rec.arts.books, rec.boats
   From: jkohnen@efn.org (John Kohnen)

On-line Book Publisher List
   Newsgroups: rec.arts.books, rec.arts.books.marketplace,
      rec.arts.books.childrens, rec.arts.mystery
   From: brock@ucsub.Colorado.edu (Steve Brock)

On-line Books FAQ
   Newsgroups: alt.etext, rec.arts.books,
      alt.internet.services, sci.classics
   From: dell@wiretap.spies.com (Thomas Dell)

On-line Bookstores List
   Newsgroups: rec.arts.books,
      rec.arts.books.marketplace,
      rec.arts.books.childrens, rec.arts.mystery
   From: brock@ucsub.Colorado.edu (Steve Brock)

Terry Prachett Bibliography
   Newsgroups: alt.fan.pratchett, news.answers,
      alt.answers
   From: gnat@kauri.vuw.ac.nz (Nathan Torkington)
   Archive name: pratchett/bibliography

Project Gutenberg List of Etext (Part I)
Project Gutenberg List of Etext (Part II)
   Newsgroups: alt.etext
   From: dircompg@sunee.uwaterloo.ca (Project
   Gutenberg)

Thomas Pynchon FAQ
   Newsgroups: rec.arts.books
   From: jorn@mcs.com (Jorn Barger)

rec.arts.books bookstores list: Cambridge/Boston
   Newsgroups: rec.arts.books
   From: nichael@bbn.com (Nichael Cramer)

rec.arts.books FAQ
   Newsgroups: rec.arts.books, rec.answers,
     news.answers
   From: ecl@mtgp003.mt.att.com (Evelyn C. Leeper)
   Archive name: books/faq

rec.arts.comics FAQ
   Newsgroups: rec.arts.comics.info,
     rec.arts.comics.misc, rec.answers, news.answers
   From: tyg@hq.ileaf.com (Tom Galloway)
   Archive name: comics/faq/part1 [-7]

rec.arts.sf groups, an introduction
   Newsgroups: rec.arts.sf.announce, rec.arts.sf.misc,
     rec.answers, news.answers
   From: felan@netcom.com (Leanne Phillips)
   Archive name: sf/groups-intro

rec.arts.sf.reviews FAQ
    Newsgroups: rec.arts.sf.reviews, rec.answers,
        news.answers
    From: djdaneh@pbhyc.pacbell.com
    Archive name: sf/reviews-faq

rec.arts.sf.written FAQ
    Newsgroups: rec.arts.sf.written, rec.arts.sf.misc,
        news.answers, rec.answers
    From: burchard@access.digex.Net (Laura
        Burchard)
    Archive name: sf/written-intro

rec.arts.sf.written.robert-jordan FAQ
    Newsgroups: rec.arts.sf.written.robert-jordan,
        rec.arts.sf.written, rec.answers, news.answers
    From: joeshaw@info1.cc.vt.edu (Joe "Uno"
        Shaw)
    Archive name: sf/robert-jordan-faq

rec.arts.theatre FAQ
    Newsgroups: rec.arts.theatre.musicals,
        rec.arts.theatre.misc, rec.arts.theatre.plays,
        rec.answers, news.answers
    From: aku@leland.Stanford.edu (Andrew Chia-Tso Ku)
    Archive name: theatre/part1 [-3]

Anne Rice FAQ
    Newsgroups: alt.books.anne-rice, alt.answers,
        news.answers
    From: Laura Ann lat13@columbia.edu

Robin Hood Booklist
    Newsgroups: rec.arts.books, rec.answers,
        news.answers
    From: tittle@netcom.com (Cindy Tittle Moore)
    Archive name: books/robin-hood

SF-references-in-music List
    Newsgroups: rec.music.misc, rec.arts.sf.misc, rec.answers,
        news.answers
    From: rsk@aspen.circ.upenn.edu (Rich Kulawiec)
    Archive name: music/sci-fi-refs

Shakespeare in Star Trek
    Newsgroups: rec.arts.startrek.misc
    From: petersm@csos.orst.edu (Marguerite Petersen)

Sherlock Holmes Booklist (FAQ)
    Newsgroups: rec.arts.books, alt.fan.holmes, alt.answers,
        rec.answers, news.answers
    From: ecl@mtgp003.mt.att.com (Evelyn C. Leeper)
    Archive name: books/holmes/list

Sherlock Holmes Illustrated
    Newsgroups: rec.arts.books, alt.fan.holmes, rec.answers,
        alt.answers, news.answers
    From: mlbm@lanl.gov (Mark Martinez)
    Archive name: books/holmes/illustrated

Star Trek: Bibliography of ST Articles/Books
    Newsgroups: rec.arts.startrek.misc
    From: wright@facl.lan.mcgill.ca (J. Wright)

Star Trek Book Guide
  Newsgroups: rec.arts.startrek.fandom, rec.answers,
    news.answers
  From: kevina@clark.Net (Kevin Atkinson)
  Author: Arnold E. van Beverhoudt, Jr.
  71777.2365@compuserve.com
  Archive name: star-trek/CS-guide/books/part1 [-2]

Superman FAQ
  Newsgroups: rec.arts.comics.info,
    rec.arts.comics.misc, alt.comics.superman
  From: davidc@leland.Stanford.edu (David Thomas
    Chappell)
  Archive name: superman-faq

Titles of Comics Collections
  Newsgroups: rec.arts.comics.strips, rec.answers,
    news.answers
  From: dkrause@hydra.acs.uci.edu (Doug Krause)
  Archive name: comics/collections

J.R.R. Tolkien: Frequently Asked Questions
  Newsgroups: rec.arts.books.tolkien, alt.fan.tolkien,
    rec.answers, alt.answers, news.answers
  From: loos@frodo.mgh.harvard.edu (William D.B.
    Loos)
  Archive name: tolkien/faq/part1 [-2]

J.R.R. Tolkien: Less Frequently Asked Questions
  Newsgroups: rec.arts.books.tolkien, alt.fan.tolkien,
    rec.answers, alt.answers, news.answers

From: loos@frodo.mgh.harvard.edu (William D.B. Loos)
Archive name: tolkien/lessfaq/part1

Zines on the Internet
Newsgroups: alt.zines, alt.etext, misc.writing, rec.mag,
alt.Internet.services, alt.answers, misc.answers, rec.answers, news.answers
From: johnl@Netcom.com (John Labovitz)
Archive name: writing/zines/part1 [-5]

ON-LINE SERVICES

CompuServe: Books in Print (GO BOOKS)

Lists current titles, books to be published within the next six months, and books that have gone out of print within the last two years. Search by subject, author, or title.

CompuServe: British Books in Print (GO BBIP)

Includes bibliographic references describing current titles, books to be published within the next six months, and those that have been classified as out of print. Information includes author, title, publisher, date of publication, edition, binding, list price in pounds sterling, and subject.

Microsoft Network: Reading Forum

A place to talk about favorite books and authors. Occasional on-line visits from famous writers.

Prodigy: Books Forum
Without doubt the best books forum on any of the major
on-line services. Excellent content and commentary, as
well as seamless integration of intelligently selected Internet resources. Moderator: Digby Diehl.

The WELL: The Books Conference
A forum to discuss all facets of books and reading.

BOOKS AND AUTHORS

Authors

GENERAL INDEXES OF AUTHORS

<u>Author, Author!</u> Links to pages devoted to a wide range
of authors and their works.
http://www.li.net/~scharf/author.html

<u>Authornet</u> Another good overview of resources devoted
to individual authors.
http://www.imgnet.com/auth/

<u>Authors Links & Info</u> Includes newer authors (e.g.,
Martin Amis, Julian Barnes) and well-organized links to
a variety of sources, interviews, etc.
**http://www.empirenet.com/~rdaeley/authors/
authors.html**

<u>Book Stacks—Author's Pen</u> Links to many authors'
pages.
http://www.books.com/scripts/author.exe

<u>Books On-line: Authors</u> A searchable index of authors.
http://www.cs.cmu.edu/Web/bookauthors.html

<u>Great Writers</u> An extensive list of writers' home pages.
http://www.xs4all.nl/~pwessel/writers.html

<u>Literary Lists</u> Lists of prizewinners in all major categories
of literary awards.
**http://compstat.wharton.upenn.edu:8001/~siler/
litlists.html**

<u>Literary Kicks</u> A page devoted to Beat authors.
http://www.charm.net/~brooklyn/LitKicks.html

USENET NEWSGROUP
   alt.books.beatgeneration

ON-LINE SERVICES

**CompuServe: Time Warner Author Forum (GO
TWAUTHOR)**
An opportunity to meet and chat with authors published
by Time Warner. Each week a different author is featured.

**CompuServe: Time Warner Trade Publishing
Display Area (GO TWEP)**
Includes Time Warner Author Forum (GO TWAUTHOR),
Time Warner Crime Forum (GO TWCRIME), and Time
Warner Electronic Publishers bookstore (GO TWB).

RESOURCES DEVOTED TO SPECIFIC AUTHORS
Most of the Web pages, Usenet newsgroups, and mailing
lists given here are created by fans of the particular writer.

A few authors (e.g., Margaret Atwood, Anne Rice, and Madison Smartt Bell) have taken an active interest in their Web sites, and Douglas Adams is known to have posted to the **alt.fan.douglas-adams** newsgroup.

Almost all of the Web pages listed here offer a short biography, a bibliography, and links to other Net resources devoted to the author of his or her genre or era.

Because this is an abbreviated list, your favorite author may not appear here, but that doesn't mean that he or she doesn't have a Web page, mailing list, or newsgroup on the Net. Just fire up one of the search engines listed on page 128 to track down the author's name. And if you find that there is, indeed, not yet a Web page, mailing list, or newsgroup for your favorite author, that simply means that it's up to you to create one.

Douglas Adams
Oxford University Douglas Adams Society
http://sable.ox.ac.uk/~dougsoc/
The Douglas Adams Worship Page
http://www.umd.umich.edu/~nhughes/dna/
Usenet newsgroup: **alt.fan.douglas-adams**

Martin Amis
http://www.empirenet.com/~daeley/authors/amis.html

Maya Angelou
http://web.msu.edu/lecture/angelou.html

Isaac Asimov
http://www.clark.net/pub/edseiler/WWW/asimov_home_page.html
Usenet newsgroup: **alt.books.isaac-asimov**

Margaret Atwood With an introduction by the author herself.
http://www.io.org/~toadaly/toc.htm

Jane Austen Information page and a fascinating presentation of *Pride and Prejudice* in hypertext.
http://uts.cc.utexas.edu/~churchh/janeinfo.html
Mailing list: **AUSTEN-L**
Mail to: **listserv@vm1.mcgill.ca**

Paul Auster
http://www.engl.virginia.edu/~jcp3q/auster.html

Julian Barnes
http://www.empirenet.com/~rdaeley/authors/barnes.html

Aphra Behn
http://ourworld.compuserve.com/homepages/r_nestvold/

Madison Smartt Bell
http://rwd.goucher.edu/~mbell/

Robert Benchley
http://www.empirenet.com/~rdaeley/authors/benchley.html

The William Blake Page Devoted to the works of the great English Romantic poet, painter, engraver, and printer. Includes writings, poetry, and art, plus links to other Blake resources on-line.
http://www.aa.net/~urizen/blake.html

André Breton
http://www.lm.com/~kalin/breton.html

The Brontës (Emily, Charlotte, and Anne)
Mailing list: **Bronte**
Mail to: **majordomo@world.std.com**

Charles Bukowski
**http://www.empirenet.com/~rdaeley/authors/
bukowski.html** or **http://realbeer.com/buk/**

William S. Burroughs Page
http://www.cs.wisc.edu/~garms/zach/b1.html or
http://www.inch.com/~ari/words1.html

Albert Camus
http://www.inch.com/~ari/words1.html

Truman Capote
**http://www.empirenet.com/~rdaeley/authors/capote.
html**

Raymond Carver
http://world.std.com/~ptc/

Louis-Ferdinand Céline
http://www.empirenet.com/~rdaeley/authors/celine.html

Miguel de Cervantes
Mailing list: **CERVNTES**
Mail to: **listserv@listserv.acns.nwu.edu**

Raymond Chandler
**http://www.empirenet.com/~rdaeley/authors/
chandler.html**

Geoffrey Chaucer
http://www.vmi.edu/~english/chaucer.html
Mailing list: **Chaucer**
Mail to: **listserv@uicvm.uic.edu**

Noam Chomsky
http://www.lbbs.org/archive/index.htm
Usenet newsgroup: **alt.fan.noam-chomsky**

Agatha Christie
**http://www.nltl.columbia.edu/users1/bkyaffe/wwwac/
achome.html**

Tom Clancy
Usenet newsgroups: **alt.books.tom-clancy, alt.fan.
tom-clancy**

Arthur C. Clarke
http://www.lsi.usp.br/~rbianchi/clarke/
Usenet newsgroup: **alt.books.arthur-clarke**

S. T. Coleridge Home Page Major works, biographical
information, and assorted materials.
http://www.lib.virginia.edu/etext/stc/Coleridge/stc.html

Wilkie Collins Appreciation Page Inventor of the modern
detective story.
http://www.ozemail.com.au/~drgrigg/wilkie.html

Stephen Crane
**http://www.en.utexas.edu/~mmaynard/Crane/crane.
html**

Michael Crichton
http://http.tamu.edu:8000/~cmc0112/crichton.html

e. e. cummings
http://www.catalog.com/mrm/poems/poems.html

Daniel Defoe
http://www.li.net/~scharf/defoe.html

Don DeLillo
**http://jefferson.village.virginia.edu/pmc/issue.194/
abstracts.194.html**

Charles Dickens
Dickens Project Home Page Scholarly papers, conferences and links to other on-line Dickens resources.
http://hum.ucsc.edu/dickens/index.html
Mailing list: **DICKNS-L**
Mail to: **listserv@ucsbvm.ucsb.edu**

Emily Dickinson Scholarly essays, links to works online, and a mailing list.
http://lal.cs.byu.edu/people/black/dickinson.html

E. L. Doctorow
http://www.msu.edu/lecture/doctorow.html

Fyodor Dostoevsky
http://grove.ufl.edu/~flask/Dostoevsky.html

Rita Dove
http://www.lib.virginia.edu/etext/fourmill/dove.html

Arthur Conan Doyle—Sherlockian Holmepage
http://watserv1.uwaterloo.ca/~credmond/sh.html
Usenet newsgroup: **alt.fan.holmes**
Mailing list: **HOUNDS-L (Sherlock Holmes Literature)**
Mail to: **listserv@kentvm.kent.edu**

Marguerite Duras
http://www.uta.fi/~trkisa/duras/duras.html

Umberto Eco
http://www.empirenet.com/~rdaeley/authors/eco.html

T. S. Eliot
http://www.next.com/~bong/eliot/index.html

Ralph Ellison
http://www.empirenet.com/~rdaeley/authors/
ellison.html

William Faulkner
http://cypress.mcsr.olemiss.edu/~egjbp/faulkner/
faulkner.html or http://www.mcsr.olemiss.edu/
~egjbp/faulkner/faulkner.html

F. Scott Fitzgerald
http://acs.tamu.edu/~jtc5085/index.htm

Ian Fleming
http://www.mcs.net/~klast/www/fleming.html

Benjamin Franklin: Glimpses of the Man
http://sln.fi.edu/franklin/rotten.html

Robert Frost
http://www.wordslam.hugo.com/frost-directory.html

Carlos Fuentes
http://www.msu.edu/lecture/fuentes.html

André Gide
http://www.lm.com/~kalin/gide.html

Allen Ginsberg
http//nickel.ucs.indiana.edu/~avigdor/poetry/
ginsberg.html

Spalding Gray
http://www.empirenet.com/~rdaeley/authors/gray.html

John Grisham
**http://www.bdd.com/athwk/bddathwk.cgi/06-19-95/
menu**

Seamus Heaney
**http://sunsite.unc.edu/dykki/poetry/heaney/
heaney-cov.html**

Robert Heinlein
http://fly.hiwaay.net/~hester/heinlein.html
Usenet newsgroup: **alt.fan.heinlein**

Joseph Heller
**http://www.empirenet.com/~rdaeley/authors/
heller.html**
or **http://www.msu.edu/lecture/heller.html**

Ernest Hemingway
**http://www.empirenet.com/~rdaeley/authors/
hemingway.html**
Hemingway Review Devoted to the study of Hemingway's works from an academic perspective, "including but not limited to gender-based, multiculturalist, and environmental perspectives; other post-structuralist methods; and historical, textual, biographical, source, and influence studies." Just what Papa would have wanted, no doubt.
http://www.dc.enews.com/magazines/hemingway/

Hermann Hesse
**http://www.empirenet.com/~rdaeley/authors/hesse.
html**
Mailing list: **HESSE-L**
Mail to: **listserv@cmsa.berkeley.edu**

Langston Hughes
http://ie.uwindsor.ca/jazz/hughes.html

Aldous Huxley
**http://www.empirenet.com/~rdaeley/authors/
huxley.html**

Eugène Ionesco
**http://www.empirenet.com/~rdaeley/authors/
ionesco.html**

John Irving
**http://www.empirenet.com/~rdaeley/authors/irving.
html**

James Joyce
Work in Progress: James Joyce in Cyberspace
http://astro.ocis.temple.edu/~callahan/joyce.html
Mailing list: **FWAKE-L** (Finnegans Wake Discussion List)
Mail to: **listserv@irlearn.bitnet**

Franz Kafka Texts, biographical material, and links to
other resources.
http://www.cowland.com/josephk/josephk.htm

William Kennedy
http://www.msu.edu/lecture/kennedy.html

Stephen King
http://www.acs.appstate.edu/~pl7714/sking–html
Usenet newsgroup: **alt.books.stephen-king**

Milan Kundera
http://www.du.edu/~staylor/kundera.html
or **http://www.georgetown.edu/irvinemj/english016/
kundera/kundera.html**

Doris Lessing
http://tile.net/lessing/index.html

Primo Levi Page Biography, bibliography, and an interview with the author.
http://inch.com/~ari/levi1.html

C. S. Lewis
http://paul.spu.edu/~loren/lewis/ or
http://www.cache.net/~john/cslewis/index.html
Usenet newsgroup: **alt.books.cs-lewis**

Wyndham Lewis
http://130.54.80.49/Lewis/Lewis.html

Jack London
Mailing list: **JACK-LONDON**
Mail to: **JACK-LONDON-REQUEST@SONOMA. EDU**

Norman Mailer
http://www.msu.edu/lecture/mailer.html

Gabriel García Marquez
http://www.empirenet.com/~rdaeley/authors/ marquez.html

Cormac McCarthy
http://pages.prodigy.com/cormac/index.htm

Terry McMillan
http://web.msu.edu/lecture/mcmillan.html

Herman Melville
http://www.melville.org/melville.htm

Arthur Miller
http://www.msu.edu/lecture/miller.html

John Milton
http://nyx10.cs.du.edu:8001/~mgrimlei/jmilton.html
John Milton Page Home page of the MILTON-L mailing list. Offers links to mailing list archives and other Milton resources on-line.
http://www.urich.edu./~creamer/milton.html
Mailing list: **MILTON-L** (John Milton List)
Mail to: **milton-request@urvax.bitnet**

Toni Morrison
http://www.en.utexas.edu/~mmaynard/Morrison/home.html

Haruki Murakami
http://www2.hawaii.edu/~bueno/HMurakami/

Vladimir Nabokov
http://www.empirenet.com/~rdaeley/authors/nabokov.html
Mailing list: **NABOKV-L**
Mail to: **listserv@ucsbvm.ucsb.edu**

Pablo Neruda
http://www.uic.edu/~pnavia/neruda.html

Joyce Carol Oates
http://www.msu.edu/lecture/oates.html
Celestial Timepiece: A Joyce Carol Oates Home Page
http://storm.usfca.edu/usf/southerr/jco.html

Dorothy Parker
http://www.phantom.com/~eponine/parker/parker2.html

Walker Percy
http://sunsite.unc.edu/wpercy/

Edgar Allan Poe's The House of Usher
http://infoweb.magi.com/~forrest/index.html

Aleksandr Pushkin
**http://polyglot.lss.wisc.edu/lss/staff/stephy/
Pushkin.html**

Thomas Pynchon
http://www.pomona.edu/pynchon/index.html
Mailing list: **PYNCHON** (Thomas Pynchon Discussion)
Mail to: **userdog1@sfu.bitnet**
Mailing list: **PYNCHON-L**
Mail to: Contact the list moderator, John K. Gilbert, at
gilbert@sfu.ca.

Anne Rice
http://www.cyserv.com/pttong/rice.html
Anne Rice's newsletter, Commotion Strange,
http//ecosys.drdr.virginia.edu/~jsm8f/
commotion.html
Usenet newsgroup: **alt.books.anne-rice**
Mailing list: **ARBOOKS** (Discussion of books by Anne
Rice)
Mail to: **LISTSERV@PSUVM.PSU.EDU**

Alain Robbe-Grillet Bibliography and other information
on the French novelist.
http://www.halfaya.org/robbegrillet/

Tom Robbins
The Tom Robbins Homepage
http://www.rain.org/~da5e/tom_robbins.html
Usenet newsgroup: **alt.fan.tom-robbins**
Mailing list: **MAGIC-L**
Mail to: **listserv@AMERICAN.Edu**

Philip Roth
http://www.msu.edu/lecture/roth.html

Salman Rushdie
http://pages.nyu.edu/~sqg4217/rushdie.html
and **http://www.empirenet.com/~rdaeley/authors/**
rushdie.html

Antoine de Saint-Exupery
http://www.sas.upenn.edu/~smfriedm/exupery/

J. D. Salinger
http://www.mass-usr.com:80/~sfoskett/jds.html

and **http://www.empirenet.com/~rdaeley/authors/salinger.html**

<u>Hubert Selby, Jr.</u>
http://www.empirenet.com/~rdaeley/authors/selby.html

<u>Anne Sexton</u>
http://www.inch.com/~ari/words1.html

<u>William Shakespeare</u>
The Shakespeare Web
The complete works in hypertext.
http://www.shakespeare.com/
<u>Shakespeare Homepage </u>The complete works, in hypertext.
http://the-tech.mit.edu/Shakespeare/works.html
Usenet newsgroup: **humanities.lit.authors.shakespeare**
Mailing list: **SHAKSPER** (Shakespeare Electronic Conference)
Mail to: **listserv@utoronto.bitnet**

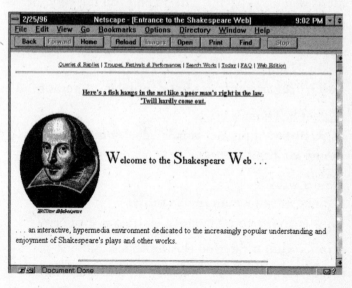

George Bernard Shaw
The Complete Shavian G. B. Shaw and his contemporaries.
http://metro.turnpike.net./T/tehart/index.html

Terry Southern
**http://www.charm.net/~brooklyn/People/
TerrySouthern.html**

Edmund Spenser
http://darkwing.uoregon.edu/~rbear/

John Steinbeck
John Steinbeck Research Center, San Jose State University
http://www.sjsu.edu/depts/steinbec/srchome.html

Robert Louis Stevenson
**http://www.efr.hw.ac.uk/EDC/edinburghers/
robert-louis-stevenson.html**

The Tennyson Page Features a timeline of Tennyson's
life as well as his poems. The graphics on this page are
gorgeous.
http://charon.sfsu.edu/TENNYSON/tennyson.html

Dylan Thomas
http://pcug.org.au/~wwhatman/dylan_thomas.html

Hunter S. Thompson
**http://www.empirenet.com/~rdaeley/authors/
thompson.html**

Alvin Toffler
Usenet newsgroup: **alt.books.toffler**

J.R.R. Tolkien
**http://csclub.uwaterloo.ca/u/relipper/tolkien/
rootpage.html**

Usenet newsgroups: **alt.fan.tolkien, rec.arts.books. tolkien**
Mailing list: **TOLKIEN**
Mail to: **listserv@jhuvm.hcf.jhu.edu**

John Kennedy Toole
http://www.empirenet.com/~rdaeley/authors/toole.html

Anthony Trollope
Mailing list: **TROLLOPE**
Mail to: **majordomo@world.std.com**

Mark Twain
http://web.syr.edu/~fjzwick/twainwww.html
Mailing list: **TWAIN-L**
Mail to: **listserv@vm1.yorku.ca**

Andrew Vachss
http://www2.hawaii.edu/~bueno/AVachss/

Kurt Vonnegut
http://www.cas.usf.edu/english/boon/vonnegut/ kv.html
Usenet newsgroup: **alt.books.kurt-vonnegut**

Derek Walcott
http://www.msu.edu/lecture/walcott.html

Evelyn Waugh
http://www.empirenet.com/~rdaeley/authors/waugh. html
or **http://home.aol.com/captgrimes**

Walt Whitman
Walt Whitman Home Page Includes his recently discov-

ered diaries, from the U.S. Library of Congress.
http://lcweb2.loc.gov/ammem/wwhome.html

Oscar Wilde
Wild Wilde Web
http://www.clients.anomtec.com/oscarwilde/

Thornton Wilder
http://www.sky.net/~emily/thornton.html

William Carlos Williams
http://www.charm.net/~brooklyn/People/
WilliamCarlos Williams. html

P. G. Wodehouse
P. G. Wodehouse Appreciation Page
http://bushrat.jpl.nasa.gov/tak/wodehouse.html
Usenet newsgroup: **alt.fan.wodehouse**

Thomas Wolfe
http://www.cms.uncwil.edu/~connelly/wolfe.html

Virginia Woolf Web
http://130.54.80.49/VW/INDEX.HTML

Children's Books and Reading Resources

Amid the media hoopla over the danger of children's accessing adult materials on the Internet, very little attention
has been given to wonderful sites designed specifically for
(and often by) children. Many children's pages have won
"Best of the Net" awards and are worth a visit, even if you
don't happen to have a child in your home. A good place to
start is:

<u>The Children's Literature Web Guide</u> Provides an excellent overview of the field.
http://www.ucalgary.ca/~dkbrown/index.html

Other notable sites include:

<u>Alice's Adventures in Wonderland</u> By Lewis Carroll, with original illustrations.
http://www.wonderland.org/Works/Lewis-Carroll/alice-in-wonderland/

<u>Anne of Avonlea</u>
http://www.cs.cmu.edu/Web/People/rgs/avontable.html

<u>Anne of the Island</u>
http://www.cs.cmu.edu/Web/People/rgs/ann-table.html

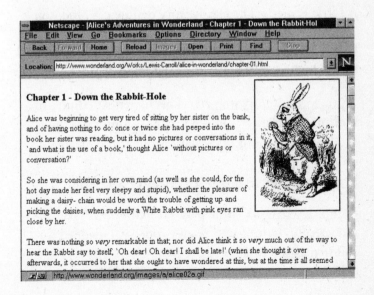

Art and Poetry Includes features on children's illustrated books and poems by children.
http://www.rrnet.com/~nakamura/ap/index.html

The Book Pile Features reviews, stories, and book lists for children ages 7 to 14. Started by Emily Stephens (age 13), who also directed the construction of the Web site.
http://www.ncf.carleton.ca/~ak001

The Frog King Hypertext The Frog King, an illustrated Grimm Brothers tale.
http://www.fln.vcu.edu/Grimm/frog.html

KidPub WWW Publishing KidPub is a place for children to publish stories on the World Wide Web and to read stories published by other children.
http://en-garde.com/kidpub/intro.html

A Little Princess The classic story by Frances Hodgson Burnett.
http://www.inform.umd.edu:8080/EdRes/Topic/ WomensStudies/ReadingRoom/Fiction/LittlePrincess

Mark Twain's Stuwwelpeter This hypertext edition of Hoffmann's classic children's story incorporates the original illustrations. Translations by Mark Twain and others.
http://www.fln.vcu.edu/Struwwel/twpete.html

Positively Poetry A home page created by a 12-year-old interested in writing and reading poetry. Designed for children ages 5 to 15.
http://iquest.com/~e-media/kv/poetry.html

Public Domain Children's Books Via Gopher
**gopher://lib.nmsu.edu/11/.subjects/Education/
.childlit/.childbooks**

Realist Wonder Society Home Page A fascinating page
featuring stories and poems for and by children.
http://www.rrnet.com/~nakamura/

Rumpelstiltskin The Grimm Brothers story, in German
and English. Original illustrations included.
http://www.fln.vcu.edu/Grimm/rumpeng.html

Scottish Folk Tales Via Gopher.
**gopher://leapfrog.almac.co.uk:70/11/scotland/
dalriada/myths/scottish**

Tales of Wonder A variety of children's tales from
around the world.
http://www.ece.ucdavis.edu/~darsie/tales.html

The Web as a Learning Tool An education-oriented
guide to the Web for educators, parents, and
children.
http://www.cs.uidaho.edu/~connie/interests.html

USENET NEWSGROUPS
   alt.arts.storytelling
   rec.arts.books
   rec.arts.books.childrens

Cultural Studies and Multicultural Literature

CWIS Listings Provides connections to academic Gopher sites devoted to African-American, Asian-American,

American Indian, Latino, and Chicano resources.
http://www.georgetown.edu/tamlit/cwis/cwis.html

Other notable sites include:

<u>African-American Literature</u> A good overview of on-line
resources.
**http://www.usc.edu/Library/Ref/Ethnic/black_lit_
main.html**

<u>Asian and Asian-American Poets</u>
http://www.rothpoem.com/asiapoet.html

<u>Asian Poets</u>
http://minerva.cis.yale.edu:80/~skyjuice/poempg.html

<u>Hispanic OnLine</u> Web site of *Hispanic* magazine, a
monthly publication for and about Hispanics.
http://www.hisp.com

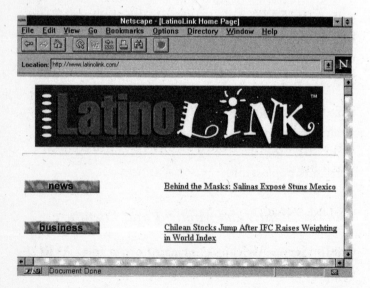

<u>Interracial Voice</u> A news journal serving the mixed-race/interracial community.
http://www.webcom.com/~intvoice/

<u>Latino Link</u> Stories, columns, and photographs by Latino journalists from the United States and Puerto Rico.
http://www.latinolink.com/

<u>Native Web</u>
http://www.maxwell.syr.edu/nativeweb/

<u>ONE</u> An African-American journal of art, music, and politics.
http://www.clark.net/pub/conquest/one/home.html

<u>Welsh Language and Culture Archive</u>
gopher://calypso.oit.unc.edu/11/sunsite.d/welsh.d

<u>The White Man's Burden and Its Critics</u> A critique of colonialism.
http://web.syr.edu/~fjzwick/kipling/whiteman.html

<u>Writing Black USA</u> Covers American black history studies and literature; includes links to source materials.
http://www.keele.ac.uk/depts/as/Literature/amlit.black.html

ON-LINE SERVICES

CompuServe: African-American Forum (GO AFRO)
Excerpts from books by important African-American au-

thors, along with articles from cultural journals. Sponsored by *American Vision* magazine.

Gay, Lesbian, and Bisexual Literature

Angel Web "A site for gay creativity including writing, poetry, and art. . . . Submissions welcome."
http://www.dircon.co.uk/angelweb

BLK Homie Pages News and information about the black lesbian and gay community.
http://www.blk.com/blk/

Christopher Street Magazine On-line version of the print magazine.
**gopher://gopher.enews.com:2100/11/magazines/
alphabetic/af/cs**

Harvard Gay and Lesbian Review
http://www.hglc.org/hglc/review.htm

InfoQueer Media Links Magazines,newspapers, etc.
http://www.infoqueer.org/queer/qis/media.html

Out Magazine On-line version of the print magazine.
http://www.out.com

OutNOW! A Northern California lesbian/gay/bisexual paper.
http://www.outnow.com

Outrageous Tokyo "Japan's first free English-language gay magazine."
**http://shrine.cyber.ad.jp/~darrell/outr/home/
outr-home.html**

PDQ News Newsletter of Digital Queers, an activist organization.
http://www.dq.org:80/dq/html/pdq/pdq.html

Queer Nasty Zine A zine dedicated to "radical thought
and intelligent humour."
http://www.tripnet.com/q-nasty/

10 Percent Magazine
**gopher://gopher.enews.com:2100/11/magazines/
alphabetic/af/tp**

Humor

Much of the humor found on-line focuses on the Internet
itself, computers, or college life. Some notable exceptions:

Canonical Collection of Tom Swifties
**http://gpu.srv.ualberta.ca/~apowell/humor/tom.
swifties.html**

Cat Bathing as a Martial Art It isn't easy. "Cats have no
handles. Add the fact that he now has soapy fur, and the
problem is radically compounded."
**http://www.castle.net/%7Etina/humordata/animals/
catwash.html**

How to Tell the Birds From the Flowers Complete text
and pictures of the Robert Woods book written in 1907.
http://cygnus.rsabbs.com/~dnewman/How/cov.html

Library Humor Humor for and about librarians, via
Gopher.
gopher://snymorva.cs.snymor.edu/ (choose "library
services," then "library humor")

Monty Python Home Page How to tell if your parrot is defunct, among other classics.
http://www.iia.org/~rosenr1/python/

News of the Weird Archive Stranger-than-fiction news stories.
http://www.nine.org/notw/archive.html

Private Eye On-line edition of the British satirical magazine.
http://www.intervid.co.uk/intervid/eye/

Pudd'nhead Wilson's Calendar by Mark Twain Maxims from the classic work; very funny.
http://web.syr.edu/~fjzwick/twain_html/maxims.html

Scott's Lardnermania "A page devoted to the memory and appreciation of sportswriter, humorist, and short story writer Ring Lardner."
http://ourworld.compuserve.com/homepages/Topping/

Shakespearean Insult Server "Thou pribbling common-kissing apple-john!" Reload the page for a new insult every time.
http://alpha.acast.nova.edu/cgi-bin/bard.pl

Tina's Humor Archives An interesting collection.
http://www.castle.net/%7Etina/fun.html

Straight Dope Archives Collection of newspaper columns by Cecil Adams.
ftp://ftp.mcs.com/mcsnet.users/krikket/tsd/
Usenet newsgroup: **alt.fan.cecil-adams**

USENET NEWSGROUPS
  alt.fan.dave-barry

alt.folklore.urban
alt.humor.puns
rec.humor
rec.humor.funny

Mystery Literature

<u>Bullets and Beer: The Spenser Page</u> For fans of the detective fiction of Robert B. Parker.
http://mirkwood.ucc.uconn.edu/spenser/spenser.html

<u>The Case—Mystery Site Links</u> A good general resource page for mystery lovers.
http://www.thecase.com/main/links.shtml

<u>ClueLass—A Mystery Newsletter</u> Excellent site for readers and aspiring writers.
http://www.slip.net/~cluelass/

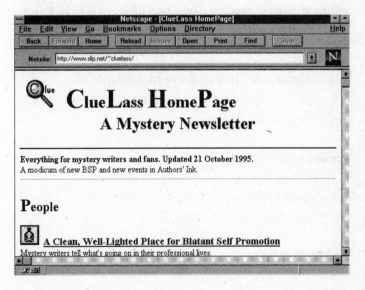

Genre Fiction: Mystery and Suspense A great resource
for lovers of detective and crime fiction.
http://www.vmedia.com/shannon/mystery.html

The Mysterious Homepage Links to anything a mystery lover
would want.
http://www.db.dk/dbaa/jbs/homepage.htm

The Mystery Zone "The first mystery magazine on the
Net." Includes stories, reviews, and links to other on-line
resources.
http://www.mindspring.com/~walter/mystzone.html

Nero Wolfe Home Page Resources for fans of Rex Stout.
**http://www.fish.com/~muffy/pages/books/rex_stout/
nero_wolfe.html**

Sherlockian Holmepage Home of all things Sherlockian.
http://watserv1.uwaterloo.ca/~credmond/sh.html

Tangled-Web British mystery site with links to authors'
home pages.
http://www.thenet.co.uk/~hickafric/tangled-web.html

221 Baker Street Another good Holmes site.
**http://www.cs.cmu.edu/afs/andrew.cmu.edu/usr18/
mset/www/holmes.html**

USENET NEWSGROUPS
   alt.fan.holmes
   bit.listserv.dorothyl
   rec.arts.mystery

ON-LINE SERVICES

The WELL: The Mystery Conference
Otherwise known as Noir, where all mystery genres are open for discussion.

Poetry Resources

There is an enormous amount of poetry on-line, not just at the sites listed here (many of which hold dozens of links to other poetry resources) but also in the growing number of e-zines, almost all of which publish verse. If you're interested in seeing your own poems published on-line, be sure to investigate the e-zines listed elsewhere in this index. For tips on putting your poems to paper, see the Writers Resources section below.

Academy of American Poets The home page of the Academy, which was founded in 1934 to support American poets at all stages of their careers and to foster the appreciation of contemporary verse. It offers information on membership, awards, and Academy programs.
http://www.he.net/~susannah/academy.htm

British Poetry 1780–1910: A Hypertext Archive An excellent collection of 19th-century poetry, much of it illustrated and annotated.
http://etext.lib.virginia.edu/britpo.html

Electronic Poetry Center Home Page A collection of poetry resources from the University of Buffalo and the Internet as a whole.
http://wings.buffalo.edu/epc/

Keats, John. 1884. Poetical Works From Columbia University's Project Bartleby.
http://www.columbia.edu/acis/bartleby/keats/

Lost Poets of the Great War The works of Rupert Brooke, Wilfred Owen, and other poets killed in World War I. A deeply moving Web site.
http://www.emory.edu/ENGLISH/Lost Poets/index.html

The New Poetry Quarterly Home Page Web site of a respected British print journal. Subscription information, poems, and index of issues on-line.
http://www.nene.ac.uk/NPQ/npqhome.html

Oscar Wilde Poems Indexed by both title and first line.
http://www.cc.columbia.edu/acis/bartleby/wilde/

Poems by Emily Dickinson The complete edition in e-text from Project Bartleby.
http://www.columbia.edu/acis/bartleby/dickinson/

Poems Poetry Poets A good collection of links to poetry resources on the Net.
http://www.execpc.com/~jon/

Poetic Express Another collective effort. The home pages of poets included are linked to this page, allowing you to jump directly to more of their poetry. Submissions welcome.
http://www.ns.net:80/~Lomar/mary3.htm

Poetry at the English Server A fine collection of poems, from Auden to Wordsworth.
http://english-www.hss.cmu.edu/poetry.html

The Poetry Garden Project An on-line communal poetry project. Many links to other poetry resources on-line.

Submissions welcome.
http://www.wwa.com/~uschwarz/poetry.html

Poetry World Home Page A variety of poetry links from around the world.
http://news.std.com/poetryworld/

The Poetry of Yeats
http://www.maths.tcd.ie/pub/yeats/Index.html

Project Bartleby E-texts of poems and writings by Frost, Keats, Millay, etc.
http://www.columbia.edu/acis/bartleby

Sandburg's Chicago Poems Via Internet Wiretap Gopher.
**gopher://wiretap.spies.com/00/Library/Classic/
chicago.txt**

Shelley, Percy Bysshe *Complete Poetical Works*, from Project Bartleby at Columbia University.
http://www.columbia.edu/acis/bartleby/shelley/

The Shiki Internet Haiku Salon Examples of haiku, information on haiku contests, and links to haiku and other poetry.
http://mikan.cc.matsuyama-u.ac.jp/~shiki/

ON-LINE SERVICES

The WELL: The Poetry Conference
Discussions cover the strengths and weaknesses of accomplished poets, favorite poetry book hit lists, references for poesy and poetic terms, fundamentals for

reading to an audience, and the political value of poetry in society.

Romance Writing

Considering that "romance literature" or "women's fiction" is one of the hottest-selling genres, it's not surprising that there are a growing number of resources on the Net for lovers of romance novels.

Romance Novels and Women's Fiction Offers a good overview of what's available on the Net.
http://www.writepage.com/romance.htm

Other notable sites include:

Rawhide and Lace A newsletter for, by, and about the women of the American West.
http://www.writepage.com/lace1.htm

Romance Author Links A directory of resources for fans of particular authors of romance novels.
http://freenet.vcu.edu/education/literature/ romauthers.html

Romance Novel Database Information on a range of romance novels.
http://www.sils.umich.edu/~sooty/romance

Romance novels also seem to inspire quite a few of their readers to write women's fiction themselves, and the Net boasts a number of resources for Romance writers.

Romance Writer's Home Page
http://www-leland.stanford.edu/~lizalee/romance/

USENET NEWSGROUP
   bit.listserv-rra-1 (Romance Readers Anonymous)

Scholarly Literary Resources

Nowhere are the academic roots of the Net more visible than in the remarkable range of scholarly resources to be found on-line. From Greek mythology to Victorian literature, the Internet offers both the casual browser and the serious researcher high-quality sources and commentary on nearly any period or type of literature. The first stop in your explorations should be:

Literary Resources on the Net An extraordinary collection of scholarly links arranged by historical period. This page was created by Jack Lynch of the University of Pennsylvania, who also maintains excellent pages devoted to English grammar and 18th-century literature (reachable through this page). It may take months to work your way through this list, but it will be time well spent.
http://www.english.upenn.edu/~jlynch/Lit/

Other notable sites include:

MYTHOLOGY

Bulfinch's Mythology The classic work in plain text via Gopher.
gopher://gopher.vt.edu:10010/11/53

<u>Joseph Campbell Foundation Web Site</u> Files and information on Joseph Campbell, the Joseph Campbell Foundation, and other resources in mythology, comparative religion, and related fields.
http://www.jcf.org/

<u>Creation Stories and Traditional Wisdom</u> This site collects different versions of creation stories from around the world.
http://www.ozemail.com.au/~reed/global/mythstor.html

<u>Encyclopedia Mystica</u> A fascinating on-line encyclopedia covering myths, legends, and folklore of all cultures. Short entries with links to other sources.
http://www.pantheon.org/myth/

<u>Myths and Legends</u> An extensive set of links to folklore and mythology resources worldwide, listed by nation and culture.
http://pubpages.unh.edu/~cbsiren/myth.html

<u>Mythtext</u> A comprehensive site covering myths of many cultures.
http://www.io.org/~untangle/mythtext.html

<u>Tales of Wonder</u> A fine collection of folk and fairy tales from Russia, Siberia, China, and North America.
http://www.ece.ucdavis.edu/~darsie/tales.html

ANCIENT AND CLASSICAL LITERATURE

Ancient World Web "The Ultimate Index of All Things Ancient."
http://atlantic.evsc.virginia.edu/julia/AW/meta.html

Latina Folia Christi Classical resources on the Net. In Latin.
http://www.umkc.edu/networking/chris/www/ languages/latin/

MEDIEVAL LITERATURE

WWW Medieval Resources Links to discussion groups, libraries, and other Web sites related to medieval resources.
http://ebbs.english.vt.edu/medieval/medieval.ebbs.html

Other notable sites include:

The Canterbury Tales Project Chaucer's classic, with illustrations.
http://www.shef.ac.uk/uni/projects/ctp/index.html

CANTUS—Database of Gregorian Chant Searchable Gopher database.
gopher://vmsgopher.cua.edu/11gopher_root_music

The Electronic Beowulf Full-color digitized images of the original manuscript.
http://www.uky.edu/ArtsSciences/English/Beowulf/

Illuminated Manuscript Images From the Bodleian Library at Oxford University.
http://rsl.ox.ac.uk/imacat.html

Images from the Book of Kells
gopher://monera.ncl.ac.uk/11/Miscellaneous/.Kells/

The Online Medieval and Classical Library A well-organized collection of public-domain medieval and classical texts.
http://sunsite.berkeley.edu/OMACL/

Piers Plowman Electronic Archive William Langland's 14th-century allegorical dream vision. Texts of all three versions.
http://jefferson.village.virginia.edu/piers/archive.goals.html

RENAISSANCE LITERATURE

Hypertext Renaissance A page devoted to the concept of hypertext as both a metaphor for, and a valuable tool in the study of, Renaissance literature.
http://www.artsci.wustl.edu/~jntolva/

Index of Shakespearean Sonnets
http://quarles.unbe.edu/shakesean/

Renaissance Electronic Texts Original texts, commentaries, and scholarly studies.
http://library.utoronto.ca/www/utel/ret/ret.html

The Renaissance on the Web An overview of Net sites devoted to Renaissance art, literature, and society.
http://www.halcyon.com/howlevin/renaissance.html

18TH-CENTURY AND ROMANTIC LITERATURE

<u>The Romantic Chronology</u> A year-by-year chronology of the Romantic Age, emphasizing the social events as well as the literature of the period.
http://humanitas.ucsb.edu/projects/pack/ rom-chrono/chrono.htm

<u>Romanticism On the Net</u> A scholarly electronic journal devoted entirely to Romantic studies. Includes articles, analyses, and links to other resources.
http://info.ox.ac.uk:80/~scat0385/

VICTORIAN LITERATURE
See also listings of individual authors, page 151.

<u>Henry Street</u> (Irish literature)
http://huizen.dds.nl/~vonb/hs-index.html

MODERN LITERATURE
See also listings of individual authors, page 151.

<u>Pulp Fiction Collection</u> (Library of Congress) Information on the library's collection of popular American fiction magazines.
http://lcweb.loc.gov/spcoll/191.html

USENET NEWSGROUPS
humanities.answers

humanities.lit.authors.shakespeare
humanities.misc

Science Fiction, Fantasy, and Horror

Judging by the remarkable number of Web pages and
Usenet newsgroups devoted to science fiction, horror,
and fantasy books and authors, these genres hold a particular fascination for the denizens of the Internet. There
is an enormous amount of material available on-line, and
many of the sites have links to workshops for the aspiring
sci-fi, horror, or fantasy writer.

SCIENCE FICTION AND FANTASY RESOURCES

Doug's SF Reviews Selections from over 200 short reviews and links to other sci-fi resources.
**http://www.astro.washington.edu/ingram/
books.html**

Espana's Science Fiction Page Primarily a listing of
authors in the science/speculative fiction field, with
bibliographies.
http://www.Catch22.COM/~espana/SFAuthors/

Feminist Science Fiction A directory of science fiction,
fantasy, and utopian fiction on the Net written from a
feminist perspective.
http://www.uic.edu/~lauramd/sf/femsf.html

Internet Top 100 SF/Fantasy List Books rated tops in periodic public voting by Internet users.
http://www.clark.net/pub/iz/Books/Top100/ top100.html

The Linköping Science Fiction and Fantasy Archive Links to a wide variety of resources from around the world.
http://sf.www.lysator.liu.se/sf_archive/sf_main.html

MIT Science Fiction Society Homepage The world's largest online collection of science fiction texts.
http://www.mit.edu:8001/activities/mitsfs/ homepage.html

Stefan Petersson's SF&Fantasy Page A very good collection of links to other sci-fi, fantasy, and horror fiction resources on the Net.
http://julmara.ce.chalmers.se/stefan/WWW/ Cyberlinks/saifai.html

Fantasy BookList An extensive list of fantasy authors and their books, including short reviews.
http://www.mcs.net/~finn/home.html

Science Fiction Authors Extensive listing of pages devoted to sci-fi authors.
http://www.oneworld.net/SF/authors/index.html

Science Fiction Omnicon A listing of characters and places in science fiction.
http://www.iinet.com.au/~fanjet/sfomain.html

Speculative Fiction Clearing House A good collection of sci-fi and fantasy resources from around the Net.
http://thule.mt.cs.cmu.edu:8001/sf-clearing-house/

Spiff's World of Science Fiction and Fantasy Another good list of authors, books, other lists, and Web pages devoted to sci-fi and fantasy.
http://http.tamu.edu:8000/~sdd2252/Docs/SciFi/ SciFi.html

Uo-Ju's Japan- and China-Related Science Fiction and Fantasy Puddle The beginnings of an index of Japan- and China-related sci-fi and fantasy resources.
http://students.vassar.edu/~crolinsk/cj-sff.html

HORROR FICTION RESOURCES

Beyond the Pale Horror, fantasy, and sci-fi reviews.
http://alf2.tcd.ie/~mmmchugh/reviews.html

DarkEcho's Web Authors, reviews, resources, and other information pertaining to horror fiction.
http://w3.gwis.com/~prlg/

Dracula Bram Stoker's classic, converted to e-text.
http://www.cs.cmu.edu/Web/People/rgs/ drac-table.html

Horror in Literature A resource page for "literary horror"—authors, links to works, and a list of what the

editor of the page considers the "100 Best Horror Novels Ever Written."
http://131.252.12.160/~caseyh/horror/book.html

RESOURCES FOR HORROR, SCIENCE FICTION, AND FANTASY WRITERS

Clique of the Tomb Beetle Horror and sci-fi zine.
http://www.tyrell.net/~rmcheal/

Science Fiction Gallery of Web Fiction A workshop for sci-fi and fantasy writers.
http://andreae.unbc.edu/williams_html/

Symphonie's Gift Magazine of science fiction, fantasy, and horror. Submissions welcome.
http://home.aol.com/SymGift

Transversions Magazine of speculative fiction, science fiction, fantasy, and horror.
http://www.astro.psu.edu/users/harlow/ transversions/

Writer Resources An on-line workshop for writers of science fiction and fantasy.
http://www.seanet.com/Users/warlock/writers.html

Writer's (Stumbling) Block Resources for horror, fantasy, and sci-fi writers.
http://alf2.tcd.ie/~mmmchugh/writer.html

USENET NEWSGROUPS

The following Usenet newsgroups cover science fiction,

fantasy, and horror fiction. Other newsgroups relating to particular authors may be found in the "Authors" section of this resource list.

alt.books.brian-lumley
alt.books.clive-barker
alt.books.dean-koontz
alt.books.deryni
alt.books.larry-niven
alt.books.m-lackey
alt.books.phil-k-dick
alt.dragons-inn
alt.fan.dragonlance
alt.drwho.creative
alt.fan.dune
alt.fan.heinlein
alt.fan.philip-dick
alt.fan.piers-anthony
alt.fan.pratchett
alt.fandom.cons
alt.fantasy.conan
alt.folklore.ghost-stories
alt.history.what-if
alt.horror
alt.horror.creative
alt.horror.cthulhu
alt.horror.werewolves
alt.tv.x-files.creative
alt.vampyres
rec.arts.sf.announce
rec.arts.sf.fandom

rec.arts.sf.marketplace
rec.arts.sf.misc
rec.arts.sf.reviews
rec.arts.sf.science
rec.arts.sf.written
rec.arts.sf.written.robert-jordan
rec.arts.startrek.reviews

ON-LINE SERVICES

CompuServe: SF Fantasy Literature Forum (GO SFLIT)

Topics in the forum include fan magazines, artwork, artists, science facts, costuming, and writing.

CompuServe: SF/Fantasy Media Forum (GO SFMEDIA)

Contains reviews of the latest in the science fiction, fantasy, and horror media. Reviews of radio and TV programs, movies, and books are included.

Microsoft Network: Science Fiction and Fantasy Forum

Discussion of science fiction, fantasy, and horror literature, including guest appearances by authors.

Prodigy: Science Fiction/Fantasy Forum

Web-based, with links to a rotating series of Web sites. Spotlights special events and announcements, updated regularly.

The WELL: Science Fiction Conference
"The WELL Science Fiction Conference is a place for readers, writers, and others to discuss any and all aspects of speculative fiction in print and media."

Theater Resources

Whether you're an actor, a playwright, a drama student, or just an avid theatergoer, the Internet is becoming a great place to find information about any aspect of the stage. Be sure to check Yahoo (**http://www.yahoo.com**) for new resources.

Drama at the English Server at Carnegie-Mellon A good list of theater resources on the Net.
http://english-www.hss.cmu.edu/drama.html

Joe Geigel's Favorite Theatre-Related Resources Another good directory of resources on the Net.
http://pscinfo.psc.edu/,geigel/menus/Theatre.html

Guide to Theater Resources on the Internet From France, an extensive list of theater resources, including information on theater-related mailing lists. In English.
http://www.ircam.fr/divers/theatre-e.html

New Dramatists Home Page New Dramatists, founded in 1949, provides a variety of resources to playwrights.
http://www.itp.tsoa.nyu.edu/~ana/ndintro.html

Off Broadway Directory of current shows.
http://artsnet.heinz.cmu.edu:80/OnBroadway

Playbill On-line On-line magazine of the New York theater community.
http://www.playbill.com

Theatre Central Theater companies, playwrights, writing
resources, and more, all neatly cataloged.
http://www.theatre-central.com

USENET NEWSGROUPS
   rec.arts.theatre
   rec.arts.theatre.misc
   rec.arts.theatre.musical
   rec.arts.theatre.plays

ON-LINE SERVICES

Microsoft Network: Theatre Forum
Forum for sharing information on theater and perfor-
mance art.

The WELL: The Theater Conference
Offers discussions on theater, opera, and perfor-
mance art.

Women's Literary Resources

For many years the Internet was known as an over-
whelmingly male domain, but the online world is
changing rapidly. The women's movement in general,
and women's studies programs at universities in particular, have begun to take advantage of the potential of

the Net for disseminating information and analysis and building virtual communities of feminist writers and scholars.

Two of the best sites devoted to women's literature give a broad overview of what's available on the Net:

Celebration of Women Writers Links to many authors and feminist texts.
http://www.cs.cmu.edu/Web/People/mmbt/women/ writers.html

Guide to Women's Literature A collection of links to resources on the Internet.
http://www.facl.mcgill.ca/guides/women.html

Other notable sites include:

Brown Women Writers Project Focusing on women's writing from roughly 1330 to 1830.
http://www.stg.brown.edu/projects/wwp/ wwp_home.html

Catt's Claws A feminist newsletter.
http://www.lm.com/women/is/cattsclaws.html

Diotima: Materials for Study of Women and Gender in the Ancient World
http://www.uky.edu/ArtsSciences/Classics/ gender.html

Feminism and Women's Studies (Carnegie-Mellon English Server) Links to women's studies resources.
http://english-www.hss.cmu.edu/Feminism.html

Girls Can Do Anything!!! A feminist e-zine (and other links).
http://www.bgsu.edu/~ckile/ckile.html

Isis: Black Women and the Arts
http://www.netdiva.com/

The Poetry of Sappho (6th–7th century B.C.)
http://www.sappho.com/poetry/sappho.htm

The Kassandra Project An introduction to German women writers, artists, and thinkers from the second half of the 18th century through the first decades of the 19th.
http://www.reed.edu/~ccampbel/tkp/

19th-Century Women Writers Web A collection of poetry, novels, and short stories, biographical material, documents, and Internet sites devoted to 19th-century American women writers.
http://clever.net/19cwww/

Victorian Women Writers Project Women writers of the late 19th century; offers background and links to works.
http://www.indiana.edu/~letrs/vwwp/

Women of Achievement and Herstory A newsletter.
http://worcester.lm.com/~women/is/achievement.html

Women in Greek Mythology Analysis of women's roles in the ancient world.
http://www.princeton.edu/~tinalee/women.html

Women's Books Online Reviews of women's books.
http://www.cybergirl.com/review

<u>Women's Studies WWW Pages and Gophers</u> An extra-
ordinary selection of links to women's studies resources.
**http://www-unix.umbc.edu/~korenman/wmst/links.
html**

<u>Women's Wire</u> A new interactive magazine for women.
http://women.com/

ONLINE SERVICES

Prodigy: Women's Connection
Dedicated to helping women "find the needles of information in the Internet haystack." Topics include art, gender
equity, magazines and publications, organizations, and
women's studies.

E-TEXTS: BOOKS ON-LINE

The following are archives of e-texts, digital versions of
entire books, usually classics not covered by copyright
and thus in the public domain. Simply because a book
is in the public domain, though, doesn't mean that
it is commonplace, and many of the texts in these
archives are lesser-known works of famous authors or
"forgotten classics" of bygone eras. Several archives also
contain digitized versions of hard-to-find Greek and
Roman classics.

Unfortunately, space considerations forbid listing
every one of the thousands of e-texts available on-line
here, but all of these archives are well organized and

many provide search facilities, so finding particular e-texts is a remarkably simple process. If you do have difficulty finding a particular text, posting a query in the *alt.etext* Usenet newsgroup will usually bring help. It's a good idea to check *alt.etext* periodically, anyway— announcements of new on-line offerings are often given there, and many writers post their own original e-texts to this group.

The e-texts in these archives are available for downloading to your home computer at no cost. It's a good idea, however, to give some thought to how long the work may be before you begin downloading it: *Moby Dick* might take several hours (possibly days) to transfer to your home computer, and if you're paying by the hour for Internet access, you'd be far better off buying a copy at a bookstore.

Probably the best place to look for e-texts is the Project Gutenberg Home Page, where you'll find an index of the thousands of works converted to e-text by the project:
http://jg.cso.uiuc.edu/PG/welcome.html
or **http://www.w3.org/hypertext/DataSources/bySubject/Literature/Gutenberg/Overview.html**

Other general sources of e-texts include:

Alex: A Catalog of Electronic Texts on the Internet
http://www.lib.ncsu.edu/stacks/alex-index.html

Alive and Free Free works from contemporary authors available on-line.
http://www.digimark.net/mfu/alivfree.html

B&R Samizdat Express Publishes "Internet on a Disk," a free newsletter announcing new e-texts on the Net. The place to look for out-of-the-ordinary e-texts.
http://www.samizdat.com/

Banned Books On-line A special exhibit of books that have been the objects of censorship and censorship attempts. Many of the books themselves are available here.
http://www.cs.cmu.edu/Web/People/spok/ banned-books.html

Books On-line, New Listings
http://www.cs.cmu.edu/Web/booknew.html

Book Stacks Library A collection of e-texts from other archives.
http://www.books.com/lib1.htm

The Eden Etext Archive A highly subjective personal archive reflecting the page owner's tastes. You'll find everything from Aesop's Fables to an episode guide for the Muppets TV show here.
http://www.cs.rmit.edu.au/etext/

Electronic Texts, Journals, Newsletters, Magazines and Collections A good overview of e-text resources available at various sites on the Net.
http://dewey.lib.ncsu.edu/stacks/index.html

Electronic Text Center—University of Virginia Links to thousands of e-texts in a variety of languages.
http://www.lib.virginia.edu/etext/ETC.html

English Language and Literature An excellent list of links to texts and other reading resources available on-line. This page is available in both English and French versions.

http://137.122.12.15/Docs/Directories/EngLitDir.html

The ETEXT Archives One of the most comprehensive e-text archives on the Net. Electronic books, zines, and informational files on a wide variety of subjects are available.

http://www.etext.org/

European Literature Lists Internet sources for literary texts in Western European languages other than English.

http://www.lib.virginia.edu/wess/etexts.html

Internet Public Library (IPL) A collection of public-domain works organized on the model of a "real" library.

http://ipl.sils.umich.edu/

Internet Wiretap Book Collection An index of e-texts maintained by Internet Wiretap, a major electronic text initiative. Includes many classics and lesser-known works.

gopher://wiretap.spies.com:70/11/Books

Net Etext Resources A good roundup of sources for e-texts.

http://www.cs.rmit.edu.au/etext/links.html

Oxford Text Archive Many obscure and rare classical texts. Check Web page for access limitations and catalog information.

http://info.ox.ac.uk/~archive

Project Bartleby The beginnings of a first-class on-line library of e-texts, from Columbia University.

http://www.columbia.edu/acis/bartleby/

<u>Quartz Archives</u> The Quartz e-text archives at Rutgers University were shut down in 1995 but live on at this site. Some quirky text material is archived here.
http://www.etext.org/Quartz/

<u>World-Wide Web Virtual Library</u> Links to all sorts of book-related resources, including a variety of sites offering on-line e-texts.
http://www.w3.org/hypertext/DataSources/ bySubject/Overview.html or
http://sunsite.unc.edu/ibic/IBIC-homepage.html

<u>WWW VL: Literature/World Literature</u>
http://sunsite.unc.edu/ibic/IBIC-World-Lit.html

More specialized collections of e-texts are available at:

<u>Bhaktivedanta Book Trust</u> Eastern religion texts.
http://www.webcom.com/~ara/col/books/

<u>Calvin College—Christian Literature on the Internet</u>
http://www.calvin.edu/Christian/pw.html/

<u>Camelot Project</u> Arthurian texts.
http://rodent.lib.rochester.edu/camelot/cphome.htm

<u>Christian Classics Ethereal Library</u>
http://ccel.wheaton.edu/

<u>Contemporary American Poetry Archives</u> An archive of out-of-print modern American poetry.
gopher://gopher.smith.edu/11/more/capa

<u>CURIA Irish Manuscript Project</u> Historical Irish texts, from Cork, Ireland.
http://curia.ucc.ie/curia/menu.html

Freethought Web Atheist and related literature.
http://freethought.tamu.edu/freethought/

Literature, Arts, and Medicine Database A database
of texts relevant to humanities education for medical
students.
**http://mchip00.med.nyu.edu/lit-med/lit-med-db/
topview.html**

Marx-Engels Archive Well-organized archive of their
major works.
http://csf.Colorado.EDU/psn/marx/

Online Medieval and Classical Library A selection of
public-domain texts.
http://sunsite.berkeley.edu/OMACL/

Perseus Project Classical Greek texts in translation.
http://www.perseus.tufts.edu/

Progetto Manuzio Italian literature (in Italian).
**http://www.dsi.unimi.it/Users/aprile/Cornucopia/
Manuzio.html**

Project Libellus Classical texts available on-line.
ftp://ftp.u.washington.edu/public/libellus

Project Runeberg Scandinavian literature.
http://www.lysator.liu.se/runeberg/Main.html

Shakespeare Homepage Links to the Bard's works.
http://the-tech.mit.edu/Shakespeare/works.html

Tech Classics Archive A beautifully designed site offering hundreds of Greek and Latin classics.
http://the-tech.mit.edu/Classics/

<u>Victorian Web Overview</u> Texts and other resources relating to late-19th-century English literature.
http://www.stg.brown.edu/projects/hypertext/landow/victorian/victov.html

USENET NEWSGROUPS
  alt.etext
  alt.hypertext
  bit.listserv-gutnberg-l

HYPERTEXT LITERATURE

Hypertext—text with embedded links that allow the reader to jump to another document or resource—is literally the foundation of the World Wide Web. While hypertext technology thus far has been used primarily to link sites, an increasing number of hypertext novels and other literature are starting to appear on the Web. Hypertext literature uses links to create a genuinely new, non-linear structure for storytelling, permitting multiple paths through a narrative. All of which just proves how hard it is to describe hypertext—better to start up your Web browser and give the future a whirl. Probably the best place to begin your exploration is a page designed specifically as an introduction to hypertext:

<u>Hyperizons: Hypertext Fiction</u> Offers many pointers to both the theory and the practice of hypertext. Includes the page formerly known as "The Search for Some Hypertext Fiction."
http://www.duke.edu/~mshumate/hyperfic.html

Once you get your feet wet, pay a visit to some examples of hypertext in action:

<u>Bordeaux and Prague</u> A collection of illustrated hypertext "fictions."
http://www.freedonia.com/~carl/bp/

<u>Delirium</u> A serial hypertext novel by Douglas Cooper.
http://pathfinder.com/twep/Features/Delirium/DelTitle.html

<u>Eastgate Systems</u> A leading publisher of both hypertext books and hypertext construction software. Their Web site offers samples of hypertext books and free trial software.
http://www.eastgate.com/

<u>UNLISTED by William H. Calvin</u> "A novel of the Internet Era" serialized on-line in hypertext.
http://www.well.com/user/wcalvin/bkf2toc.html

USENET NEWSGROUP
   alt.hypertext

BOOKSTORES AND PUBLISHERS

BOOKSTORES
The bookstores listed here accept orders via e-mail, and some also have facilities for taking credit card orders through their Web pages. If you're looking for a particularly obscure or out-of-print book and can't find it at one of these on-line sites, post a request in the **rec.arts.books.marketplace** Usenet newsgroup.

Probably the best place to look for general information about booksellers on the Net is:

American Booksellers Association—BookWeb Home Page Links to hundreds of booksellers and publishers, as well as to literary resources around the world.
http://www.ambook.org/bookweb/

Other general indexes of bookstores on-line include:

Bookseller Lists
http://www.ambook.org/bookweb/sellerlist/

BookWire "The First Place to Look for Book Information." Well, one of the first places, anyway. Includes a list of on-line bookstores and publishers.
http://www.bookwire.com/

The World-Wide Web Virtual Library: Publishers/Bookstores Another good list of on-line booksellers.
http://www.comlab.ox.ac.uk/archive/publishers/ bookstores.html

Some specific bookstore sites you might like to visit include:

Amazon Books Claims to carry 1.1 million titles and features a handy personal notification service, which will keep you abreast of new titles in your fields of interest.
http://www.amazon.com/

Basement Full of Books New books, available by mail directly from their authors.
http://www.cis.ohio-state.edu/hypertext/faq/usenet/ books/basement-full-of-books/faq.html

Blackwell's Bookshops "England's finest academic book-seller." On-line search of their huge catalog is available.
http://www.blackwell.co.uk/bookshops/

The Bookplex A chatty bookstore/resource site that seems to want to remind customers of a shopping mall.
http://www.gigaplex.com/books/index.htm

BookZONE A very good on-line bookstore. Browse their electronic aisles or search for books by keyword. You can also search for an old-fashioned "physical" bookstore in your area.
http://ttx.com/bookzone/

Bunch of Grapes Bookstore Inc. A nice little bookstore on Martha's Vineyard, Mass. Browse reviews by the store's staff and order books over the Net. A good example of smaller bookstores utilizing the power of the Net to make geography irrelevant.
http://pleasant.cambridge.ma.us/biz/bunchgr

City Lights Publishers and Booksellers The classic San Francisco bookstore/publishing house, on-line. Complete catalog and ordering information available.
http://www.town.hall.org/places/city_lights/

A Clean Well-Lighted Place for Books Web site of a small chain of bookstores in California. Read book reviews by the stores' staff, post your own comments, or just browse the catalog.
http://www.bookstore.com/

The Internet Book Shop Claims a "virtual inventory" of more than 780,000 books. This really just means that they'll order anything you want, but since they're in the

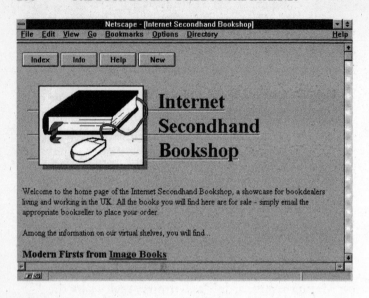

U.K., this is the place to look for books from Britain.
http://www.bookshop.co.uk/

Internet Secondhand Bookshop A showcase for used
book dealers in the U.K.
http://www.cityscape.co.uk/users/ds

Kenny's Bookshop Home Page A wonderful bookshop
in Galway, Ireland. Their sophisticated search engine
will find books you never knew existed.
http://www.iol.ie/resource/kennys/

The Native Book Centre Offers Native American books
and related materials for order on-line.
http://www.9to5.com/9to5/NBC/

The Virtual Bookstore More than 65,000 titles available.
Searchable catalog and ordering information on-line.
http://www.literascape.com/Duthie/VirtBook/

<u>Virtual Moe's</u> The on-line home of the quintessential independent bookstore in Berkeley, Calif.
http://moesbooks.com/moes.htm

<u>Virtual WordsWorth</u> Superbly designed home page of a discount bookseller in Cambridge, Mass. Offers catalog search, on-line events, discussion areas, extensive links to other book-related sites, and more.
http://www.wordsworth.com/

USENET NEWSGROUPS
  rec.arts.books
  rec arts.books.marketplace

Publishers

Most major (and many smaller) publishers now have at least a basic Web page on-line. Many allow you to search their catalogs, and several will invite you to browse sample chapters of their current bestsellers. Some general indexes of publishers on-line include:

<u>Bookwire Index of Publishers</u> Links to more than 600 publishers, neatly indexed.
http://www.bookwire.com/index/publishers.html

<u>Publishers' Catalogs Home Pages</u> A comprehensive list of publishers worldwide.
http://www.lights.com/publisher/

<u>The Small Press Net</u> A list of links to small presses.
http://www.io.org/~gutter/#spn

Just about any publisher, large or small, can be found on one of the above indexes.

For a sense of what a few of the larger publishers are up to on-line, pay a visit to some of these sites:

Bantam Doubleday Dell Online
http://www.bdd.com/

Houghton Mifflin
http://www.hmco.com/

J. B. Lippincott
gopher://infx.infor.com:5200/1

Little, Brown
http://pathfinder.com/twep/Little_Brown/Little_ Brown.html

McGraw-Hill
gopher://ns1.infor.COM:5000/1

Oxford University Press
http://www.oup.co.uk

Penguin Books
http://www.penguin.com/usa/

Princeton University Press
gopher://aaup.pupress.princeton.edu:70/11/

Random House
http://www.randomhouse.com/

For a sample of some of the more unusual publishers on-line, try a visit to these:

Black Ice Books The publishers who claim to have invented the "avant-pop" genre.
http://marketplace.com/alt.x/black.ice.books.html

Blue Heron Publishing Children's books and books about writing.
http://www.teleport.com/~bhp/

Cedar Bay Press Publishes *Literary Fragments Magazine*, nonfiction and fiction by new authors.
http://www.teleport.com/~cedarbay/index.html

Circlet Press Publishes erotic science fiction and fantasy.
http://www.apocalypse.org/circlet/home.html

Coyote Cowboy Company Humorous poetry and prose by Baxter Black, the cowboy poet.
http://www.ReadersNdex.com/coyote

Dunce Directive Publishes books on popular culture and music.
http://www.demon.co.uk/london-calling/dunce.html

Goose Lane Editions Fiction, nonfiction, poetry, and essays, primarily on Canadian subjects.
http://www.cygnus.nb.ca/glane/glogo.html

Gutter Press Publishes "dangerous fiction and radical literature."
http://www.io.org/~gutter/

Manic D Press Publishes contemporary fiction and poetry.
http://www.well.com/user/manicd/

Nolo Press Publishes self-help legal reference works.
http://gnn.com/gnn/bus/nolo/

Pinon Publishing Company Humor books. Publishers of
Beginning Farming and *What Makes a Sheep Tick.*
http://www.qinet.com/pinon/

Purple Paradox Press Publishers of *Be Your Own Thera-
pist*, a self-help book for "the person of average mental
health."
http://www.slip.net/~purplepp

Spunk Press Publishers of anarchist books, etc.
http://www.cwi.nl/cwi/people/Jack.Jansen/spunk/
Spunk_Home.html

Zino Press Children's Books Publishers of high-quality
rhyming and multicultural books designed to teach
kindness and tolerance.
http://www.ku.com/zino1.html

E-zine, Magazine, and Newspaper Book Reviews

Book reviews, like everything else on the Net, vary wide-
ly in quality and scope. Some are on-line versions of
print publications, others are the informal collective efforts of Net book lovers, and at least one on-line review
consists entirely of the opinions of a lone, albeit well-
read, book lover. Many on-line book reviews welcome
submissions—just check the site itself for instructions.
Of course, you can always join hundreds of your fellow

Netters and post your review to the *rec.arts.books.reviews* or *alt.books.reviews* Usenet newsgroups.

The Boston Book Review An excellent Web version of a prestigious print literary review. Search by title, author, or subject.
http://www.bookwire.com/bbr/bbr-home.html

Danny Yee's Book Reviews Hundreds of book reviews, all by Danny Yee. Danny reads a lot.
http://www.anatomy.su.oz.au/danny/book-reviews/index.html

Hungry Mind Home Page An excellent independent book review from the bookstore of the same name in St. Paul, Minn. Offers reviews, discussion areas, a newsletter and lots more. One of the best sites on the Web, period.
http://www.bookwire.com/hmr/homepage.html

The Quarterly Black Review of Books Excellent Web version of a print review focusing on fiction, nonfiction, and poetry of special interest to the African-American community.
http://www.bookwire.com/qbr/qbr.html

Reviews from the Forbidden Planet Reviews of sci-fi and fantasy books.
http://www.maths.tcd.ie/mmm/index.html

WWW VL: Literature/IBIC Virtual Review of Books A collection of links to both general-interest and specialized book reviews available on-line.
http://sunsite.unc.edu/ibic/IVRB.html

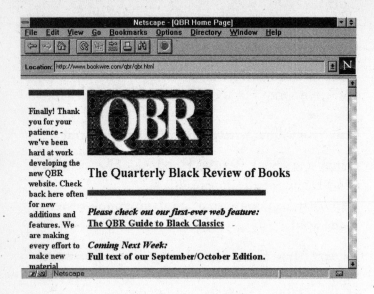

USENET NEWSGROUPS
   alt.books.reviews
   rec.arts.books.reviews

ON-LINE SERVICES

CompuServe: Book Review Digest (GO BOOKREVIEW)
Book Review Digest provides references to fiction and nonfiction English language books. Reviews are drawn from American, Canadian, and British periodicals covering general and social sciences, humanities, and reference. The digest maintains a full citation and abstract for each book.

CompuServe: UK Book Reviews (GO UKBOOKS)

Contains details of the top 10 hardback and paperback books currently available in the U.K.

E-zines and Literary Journals

E-zines (electronic magazines) on the Net range from the absolutely fascinating to the utterly puzzling. Fortunately, there are an enormous number of e-zines from which to choose, and new ones crop up every day on the Net. Probably the best starting point for a journey into zine-land is:

John Labovitz's E-zine-list Considered the best index of e-zines on-line.
http://www.meer.net/~johnl/e-zine-list/index.html

Other good indexes of e-zines can be found at:

EJournals Another good directory of e-zines.
http://137.122.12.15/Docs/EJournals.html

Electronic Journals Yet another directory of e-zines, but it lists at least one or two zines the other directories have missed.
http://www.edoc.com/ejournal/

Electronic Magazines Neatly catalogs hundreds of e-zines.
http://www.etext.org/Zines/

E-Zine Reviews
http://sunsite.unc.edu/faint/eziner/index.html

FactSheet Five Web site of a well-known index of print zines.
http://kzsu.stanford.edu/uwi/f5e/f5e.html

The e-zine explosion has brought with it a profusion of on-line literary journals, in many cases combining the irreverent sensibility of an e-zine with a focus on literature and writing. The following list is a sampling of some of the hundreds of literary zines on-line. Many of these journals welcome submissions from readers—check the particular site for details.

In general, e-zines are aimed at a young, "avant-pop" audience, so many mix original stories and poems, book and record reviews, and critiques of popular culture with political tracts of a vaguely anarchist bent. Many e-zines are also laden with large graphics, which can make loading them into your browser a painfully slow process, so you may wish to set your browser to "no graphics" before you start exploring.

Abraxus Reader A "reader-customizable" site: visitors choose what they want to see on subsequent visits. Fiction, poetry, etc. Accepts submissions.
http://www.virtumell.com/zines/vidiot

The Acid-Free Paper Fine art, literature, and Net culture. Welcomes submissions. A graphically elaborate site (which is a nice way of saying that it takes forever to load in your browser).
http://tnt.vianet.on.ca/pages/smithk

<u>Alt-X</u> The *Utne Reader* called it "an insurgent cell in the heart of the vast digicosmos of corporate info-spamming and vapid techno-babble," but judge for yourself. Offers poetry, fiction, and essays. Another graphically elaborate site, but there's a text-only version available for the impatient.
http://www.altx.com/

<u>Alter Ego</u> An excellent zine put together by students at Mt. Rainier High School in Des Moines, Wash. Serious fiction and art—very impressive.
http://www.seanet.com/Users/ianzm/
alterego.html

<u>Angel Exhaust</u> Poetry—quite a lot of it. Submissions accepted.
http://angel-exhaust.offworld.org

<u>Art Bin</u> From Sweden, with an emphasis on art and essays on art.
http://www.algonet.se/artbin/

<u>Atmospherics</u> Text-only e-zine published by a librarian in Toronto. Mostly free-form poetry.
http://www.inforamp.net/~billie/

<u>Bakunin</u> "A literary magazine for the dead Russian anarchist in all of us." Fiction, poetry, and essays, with a nondoctrinaire leftist bent. Accepts submissions.
http://www.execpc.com/~biblogic/bakunin/
index.html

Basilisk Quarterly on-line journal of film, architecture, philosophy, literature, and music. A beautifully designed site. Content tends toward the scholarly.
http://swerve.basilisk.com/

Beatrice Nonfiction, essays, book reviews.
http://www.primenet.com/~grifter/beatrice.html

beatthief Showcases "plagiarism, shoplifting, blackmail, and perjury." All in the name (and form) of poetry, of course.
http://www.beatthief.com/

blood + aphorisms A serious on-line journal of fiction. Accepts submissions and awards prizes.
http://www.io.org/~blood

Blue Penny Quarterly A high-quality literary fiction and poetry journal produced by the English Department of the College of Arts and Sciences at Virginia Tech. Accepts submissions, but the competition is stiff.
http://ebbs.english.vt.edu/olp/bpq/front-page.html

bOING bOING Cheerful Web site of a popular print zine. Culture, music, reviews of other zines.
http://www.zeitgeist.net/Public/Boing-boing/boing.boing.html

Books 2 Read Actually an on-line book club/magazine (membership free). The Web page features articles about fiction, reviews of books, and interviews with authors. The site also hosts on-line reading groups and offers discounts to members on book purchases.
http://www.b2r.com

Brazen Orality Largely poetry, evidently fueled by far too much caffeine. "Submissions of any and all stripes are encouraged, foamingly so in fact, but that's altogether up to you."
http://www.infobahnos.com/~brazen/

Breakfast Surreal Bills itself as "The Mutating Online Journal of Modern Poetry." Actually a list of links to poetry on other people's home pages. If you have a home page with poetry on it, submit it to the editor.
http://www.indirect.com/user/warren/surreal.html

Brink Conceptual poetry. An acquired taste. Accepts submissions.
http://brink.com/brink/

BVI-Web Features "experiential, political, and other writings from authors around the world." An interesting selection of essays from various cultures.
http://www.wln.com/~bensonj/bvi.html

Caffeine Magazine Fiction, poetry, and essays with a Beat bent. Offers a handy form to upload your own creations.
http://hallucinet.com/caffeine

Cat Machine Short fiction and poetry. Welcomes submissions. Apparently has absolutely nothing to do with cats.
http://www.students.uiuc.edu/~wiberg/cat/

Change Magazine Poetry, fiction, and essays focusing on environmental issues, broadly defined, not didactic.

http://www.woodwind.com/imaja/Change/ChangeMagazine.html

<u>Cliche</u> "Poetry and prose from people who are not refrigerators." Uh, OK. Submissions from nonappliances welcome.
http://www.mbhs.edu/~dchase/cliche.html

<u>Coelacanth</u> "Coelacanth is a webzine that sets out to do things differently, to challenge the reader with writing that defies convention." Actually a fairly conventional Web zine. Poetry, fiction, journals, and essays.
http://members.gnn.com/xerickson/zine.htm

<u>CrossConnect</u> A fairly straight triannual electronic journal for contemporary art and writing based at the University of Pennsylvania in Philadelphia. Accepts submissions.
http://tech1.dccs.upenn.edu/~xconnect/

<u>Cyberkind</u> "Literature for a wired age." Accepts short fiction, essays, and artwork as long as the material has something to do with the Internet or computers in general.
http://sunsite.unc.edu/shannon/ckind/toc.html

<u>CyberMom Dot Com</u> Provides a warm and homey feeling, complete with recipes.
http://www.thecybermom.com/

<u>Cybersphere</u> French Web zine dedicated to cyberculture and the information age. Published monthly. Bilingual English/French.
http://www.quelm.fr/CybersphereU.html

DargonZine Collaborative fantasy fiction by aspiring writers. Submissions are encouraged (after all, they're the
whole point of this zine).
http://www.shore.net/~dargon/

dEPARTUREfROMnORMAL Putting it mildly.
Short fiction and lots of artwork. Welcomes
submissions.
http://www.teleport.com/~xwinds/dfn.html

Depth Probe "A Web-zine about modern culture in
America." Hint: They're not thrilled with it. Essays on a
variety of subjects.
http://www.atdesign.com/~ake/

Echoes Magazine Poetry, essays, and fiction. An un-
usually energetic, cheerfully positive zine. Submissions
welcome.
http://users.aol.com/echoesmag/

Edifice of Writing and Literature A very stylish site.
Publishes theme issues (sci-fi, GenX), so check writers'
guidelines before submitting material.
http://www-leland.stanford.edu/~lmgorbea/

Electronic Darpan A literary magazine devoted to reflec-
tions on India, published by students at the University
of Illinois at Urbana-Champaign.
http://www.sponser.net/~pmishra/darpan/

Enormous Sky Poetry, prose, artwork, and photography
produced by the students of Temple University.
http://www.music.temple.edu/Sky/

Enterprise City A virtual city that visitors can explore while reading snippets of fiction along the way. Hours of wandering fun, if you have the time.
http://www.thebook.com/enterprise/city.htm

Enterzone Poetry, fiction, essays.
http://enterzone.berkeley.edu/enterzone.html

E-scape "The digital journal of speculative fiction." Publishes science fiction, fantasy, and horror. Submissions welcome. Magazine is in Adobe PDF format, requiring Acrobat reader software, available free at site.
http://www.interink.com/escape.html

eScene Yearly anthology of the "best on-line-published short fiction" from other e-zines on the Internet. Available in a variety of formats (PDF, ASCII, etc.). Submissions not accepted—work must be published elsewhere first.
http://www.etext.org/Zines/eScene/

@EZine Poetry, fiction, and humor—quite an ambitious site.
http://home.ptd.net/~vitter/@ezine.htm

Far Gone Web site of a print literary magazine. Interviews with Ken Kesey and Timothy Leary.
http://www.ucs.usl.edu/~tbf4931/fargone.html

15 Credibility Street Original fiction, poetry, and artwork. Considered one of the best Web sites. Accepts submissions.
http://socsci.smith.edu/tmbxweb/15cst/15cst.htm

5IVE Candles "5IVE Candles is a magazine that seeks to exploit the non-linear qualities of Hypertext to create a

stimulating experience." And what could be more stimulating than starting a word with a number?
**http://www.facl.mcgill.ca/courses/engl378/socks/
Welcome.html**

Flatland Sponsored by a print publisher of fringe
material. Heavily into Wilhelm Reich and flying
saucers.
**http://www.mcn.org/cbc/Bussect/Flatland/
flatland.html**

Fryburger Fiction, poetry, and essays from Freiburg,
Germany. In English. Eager for submissions.
**http://www.uni-freiburg.de/borsch/fryburger/
fryburger.html**

Fugue University of Idaho literary digest. Fiction,
poetry, and interviews. Features high-profile writers, but
welcomes submissions.
http://www.uidaho.edu/LS/Eng/Fugue

Gargoyle Magazine The student-run humor magazine of the University of Michigan. Welcomes
submissions.
http://www.pub.umich.edu/garg/index.html

Garrett County Journal Fiction, poetry, etc. Self-
consciously cool layout, pedestrian content.
http://www.cyborganic.com/People/garrett/

Geekgirl The world's first cyberfeminist zine. Essays and
interviews.
http://www.next.com.au/spyfood/geekgirl/

<u>Gerbil</u> A quarterly "Queer culture zine." Prose, poetry, fiction, nonfiction, and interviews.
http://www.multicom.org/gerbil/gerbil.htm

<u>Glimmer Train Press</u> Web site of a quarterly print short story journal. Some stories available on-line.
http://glimmertrain.com/

<u>Gothic Journal</u> The Web site of a print "news and review magazine for readers, writers, and publishers of romantic suspense, romantic mystery, and gothic, supernatural, and woman-in-jeopardy romance novels." Woman-in-jeopardy novels? Reviews, sample articles available on-line.
http://gothicjournal.com/romance/

<u>Grilled Pterodactyl</u> A one-man production—periodic ruminations on life, computers, and all the rest from a longtime fanzine publisher in Australia.
http://www.ozemail.com.au/~drgrigg/ ptero.html

<u>Harvard Advocate Home Page</u> High-caliber poetry, fiction, and essays. Accepts submissions.
http://hcs.harvard.edu:80/~advocate/

<u>Hawk</u> A quarterly journal of art and writing. Snazzy graphics.
http://www.cruzio.com/~hawk/

<u>Highbeams</u> Literary quarterly from Beloit College. Submissions welcome.
http://stu.beloit.edu/~highbe/

h2so4 Sulfuric acid, in case you were wondering. Fiction and poetry from a print zine.
http://weber.u.washington.edu/~acidic/h2so4.html

i like monkeys Short, unusual stories. Submissions welcome.
http://thumper.pomona.edu/~parango/monkeys/

Interbang Poetry, fiction, articles, and essays, and they'd like to see yours, too. An "interbang," it seems, is a combination of a question mark and an exclamation point, and is said to be a typical reaction to the articles here.
http://www.azc.com/client/bertye/

InterText: Online Fiction Magazine One of the oldest zines on-line (1991). Publishes both general fiction and science fiction/horror. Submissions welcome.
http://ftp.etext.org/Zines/InterText/intertext.html

In Vivo Literary Magazine Interesting on-line literary journal. Encourages submissions, and offers the helpful Internet Writer's Guidelines Listing, a searchable roundup of the submissions policies of a variety of Web zines.
http://freenet3.scri.fsu.edu:81/users/jtillman/titlepage.html

io A stylish but substantial (an all-too-rare combination) literary journal. Reviews and interviews with the likes of Spalding Gray and Kathy Acker. Submissions welcome.
http://www.altx.com/io/

Karma Lap Electronic Paper Web page of a print zine of new writing. Largely music-oriented.
http://wonka.acns.nwu.edu/~hrow/kl-e/intro.html

Konzepte New writing in German, from Berlin.
http://www.cs.tu-berlin.de/~nop/konzepte/

Kudzu: A Digital Quarterly An excellent on-line review offering literary fiction, poetry, and essays. Accepts submissions.
http://www.etext.org/Zines/Kudzu/
gopher://gopher.etext.org/11/Zines/Kudzu
ftp://ftp.etext.org/pub/Zines/Kudzu/

Kyosaku "Kyosaku is a quarterly publication dedicated to fostering a healthy zeal for poetry, humor, beauty, and life in an age when many are all too prepared to shove Art's fat ass out the door and curl up with dopey New Age shinola or turn on Hard Copy." Can't argue with that. A delightfully silly zine.
http://www.cs.oberlin.edu/students/djacobs/kyo/
kyomain.html

La Revista de Libros Avant-pop literary review from Mexico. In Spanish.
http://hardy.fciencias.unam.mx/~jp/revista.html

Liberty Tree A media review dedicated to true freedom of the press and speech. Accepts submissions of essays and articles.
http://www.prairienet.org/libertytree/

Linenoiz Cyberpunk-oriented essays and reviews.
http://www.magi.com/~vektor/linenoiz.html

Lip Service Magazine Publishes poetry, prose, and essays. Submissions welcome.
http://www.slip.net/~bhaynes/lipserv.html

<u>Literary Times</u> The Web site of a print magazine that reviews romantic fiction. Not much content, but lovely pictures of flowers.
http://www.tlt.com/

<u>Living Poets</u> E-journal of an e-mail poetry society in Derby, England. Submissions via e-mail group; information on the Web page.
http://dougal.derby.ac.uk/lpoets/

<u>Maple Syrup Simmering</u> Short stories and poetry, especially focusing on Canadian culture, although open to submissions from outside Canada.
http://web.idirect.com/~canuck/canzine.html

<u>Mississippi Review</u> An on-line monthly magazine publishing the best of literary fiction, poetry, essays, commentary, and reviews. Winner of the 1995 GNN Best of the Net Award in Literature.
http://sushi.st.usm.edu/~barthelm

<u>Missouri Review</u> From the University of Missouri, a serious Web literary review, offering reviews, essays, fiction, and poetry. Submissions welcome.
http://www.missouri.edu/~moreview/

<u>Morpo Review</u> An excellent creative Web review, featuring fiction, poetry, reviews, and more, including on-line literary discussions.
http://morpo.creighton.edu/morpo/

<u>Nemesis</u> A self-described "underground literary journal." Its statement of purpose is riddled with typographical

errors, but if that bothers you, you're probably not the intended audience anyway.
http://www.csulb.edu/~gifford/

Netherwords Poetry.
http://cobweb.utcc.utk.edu/~velazque

obscure "The quirky journal of unapologetic creativity." Enigmatic poetry with titles such as "Amish Sex Hotel." Lack of pretension saves this site; worth a look. Submissions welcome.
http://whamcat.com/obscure/

Open Scroll Publishes short fiction and poetry "in the pursuit of passion, brilliance, and insanity." Submissions welcome.
http://www.hooked.net/users/scroll/

Oyster Boy Review A literary magazine published in Chapel Hill, N.C. Fiction, poetry, and essays.
http://sunsite.unc.edu/ob/

Pandora's Box Web page of a print subscription zine from the U.K. Submissions welcome. Poetry, fiction.
http://www.tardis.ed.ac.uk/~gjed/mellissa/index.html

paperplates Web page of a print subscription zine from Canada. Poetry, fiction, essays. Submissions welcome.
http://www.hookup.net/~beekelly/

Persica Interactive Literary E-Zine Fiction, art, poetry, prose, and some nice recipes.
http://plant.peachweb.com/persica/

<u>Pif</u> Well-designed Web zine showcasing new fiction and poetry, most of it, unfortunately, very bad. Submissions welcome.
http://www.aloha.net/~lucks/pif/coming.html

<u>Postmodern Culture</u> Full text of journal of scholarly literary criticism; issues dating back to 1990 are available on-line. Sample theme: "Dynamic and Thermodynamic Tropes of the Subject in Freud and in Deleuze and Guattari."
http://jefferson.village.virginia.edu/pmc/ contents.all.html

<u>Practice</u> A prose-oriented literary magazine from Vassar College. Submissions welcome.
http://sitcom.vassar.edu/~misuba/PracticeWeb/ index.html

<u>Prism International</u> Web edition of a print literary magazine from Canada. Fiction, poetry, and essays. Submissions welcome, cash prizes (!) awarded.
http://edziza.arts.ubc.ca/crwr/prism/prism.html

<u>Proust Said That</u> He sure did. Home base for all things Proustian, mostly essays. This site is produced by the Marcel Proust Support Group of San Francisco and has an oddly charming atmosphere.
http://www.well.com/www/vision/proust

<u>Puck Magazine</u> Web site of a print literary journal— "The Unofficial Journal of the Irrepressible." Samples of poetry, fiction, interviews, and essays available on-line. Submissions to the print journal are encouraged.
http://www.armory.com/~jay/puck.html

Quanta Magazine An on-line magazine of science fiction and fantasy. Full-text search of all stories available.
http://www.etext.org/Zines/Quanta/

Recursive Angel Experimental poetry, fiction, and art. Welcomes submissions.
http://www.calldei.com/~recangel/

Richmond Review An excellent on-line literary magazine from the U.K. Fiction, poetry, and essays. Reviews of current books and extensive archives.
http://www.demon.co.uk/review/

The River Literary journal with a special fondness for essays on sports. Accepts submissions.
http://www.concom.com/~pparker/

RUNE-MIT Journal of Arts and Letters Poetry, art, and prose from the Massachusetts Institute of Technology.
http://www.ai.mit.edu/~spraxlo/rune/RUNE.html

Sensitive Skin Electronic Fiction and Review "The magazine of art and literature for people who just don't care about art and literature anymore!" But people here must care, since they've produced a very fine on-line edition of a serious print literary review.
http://www.bway.net/~sskin/

Shangri-La Seems to be a nice literary zine just getting off the ground (according to the page counter, I was visitor number 182). Eager for submissions.
http://users1.ee.net/raven/zine.htm

Sour Grapes Online Literary Magazine A well-designed and substantial literary journal. Prose, poetry, and art.

Submissions welcomed.
http://www.bdt.com/home/brianhill/created/

Sparks "Fiction, poetry, essays, experimental, political
(left wing), and other artistic miscellanea." Complete
back issues available on-line. Submissions welcome.
http://www.artsci.wustl.edu/~jmesch/sparkspage.html

Sponge Stands for "Simple People Opposing Neverend-
ing Gaudy Endeavors." Evidently considers Douglas
Adams a minor deity. Inexplicable.
http://olympia.ucr.edu/~sponge

Spout Poetry Magazine From Huddersfield, England.
Publishes only the output of a poetry workshop there,
so if you like this page, perhaps you'd best move to
Huddersfield.
**http://www.cs.man.ac.uk/peve/Staff/Jon/Poetry/
spout.html**

Standards Dedicated to promoting a multicultural analysis of society. Poetry, essays, interviews, and fiction. A visually striking site, but the actual content is a bit tedious.
http://stripe.Colorado.EDU/~standard/

Stanford Humanities Review Web site of an academic
review. Interesting, if largely theoretical, content.
http://shr.stanford.edu/shreview/index.html

Stange's Nebula An interesting Web reincarnation of the
defunct Canadian literary magazine *Nebula* (1975–
1983). Each issue contains a single long feature. Back issues available on-line.
http://www.wp.com/nebula/

State of unBeing "A collection of thought-provoking writing and literary trash." Ratio of the latter to the former seems very high. Extensive archives of past issues available on-line.
http://www.io.com/~hagbard/sob.html

Super AM Magazine "The journal for the science of leisure and the technology of art." A mildly bizarre site, featuring poetry, prose, and fat-free recipes.
http://www.superam.com/

Swagazine Rack Fiction, poetry, and prose culled from the writings of subscribers to the Swagland BBS, a local bulletin board system in Santa Barbara, Calif.
http://www.silcom.com/~zeylan/swagazine/

Swiftsure Weekly Features reviews of books published by small presses.
http://www.swifty.com/SW/

Texture A new, pleasantly unpretentious on-line monthly literary magazine. Submissions encouraged—poetry, essays, fiction, and humor.
http://catalog.com/texture/index.htm

Think Thank Thunk Art, poetry, and fiction, which they spell "fik-shun."
http://www.mediaguru.com/ttt/

Treeline: Canadian Writing on the Net A beautifully produced and innovative literary magazine with high-quality content. Poetry, fiction, essays, and art. Lists current literary contests and events. A first-rate Web resource for readers and writers.
http://130.179.92.25/Treeline/Treeline.html

<u>Trincoll Journal</u> A weekly multimedia arts journal. Published since 1992 entirely by college students.
http://www.trincoll.edu/tj/trincolljournal.html

<u>256 Shades of Grey</u> Eau Claire, Wisconsin's avant-pop literary/arts zine. Accepts poetry, fiction, essays, nonfiction, music reviews, etc.
http://www.primenet.com/~blkgrnt/index.html

<u>Underground Review</u> Calls itself "a smorgasbord of juicy stuff from the politically incorrect underground." Uh, not quite. Actually the product of a far-right outfit connected to The Gun Owners of America. Features reviews of obscure right-wing newsletters.
http://www.ionet.net/~ordway

<u>Unit Circle</u> "Your one-stop alternative culture shop." Art, fiction, poetry, music, and book reviews. Submissions welcome.
http://www.etext.org:80/Zines/UnitCircle/

<u>Urban Desires</u> The *New York Times* calls it "one of the most polished, hippest magazines on the Web, with imaginative, often interactive, art projects." Art, fiction, cultural criticism. Always something interesting.
http://www.desires.com

<u>Verbal Abuse</u> Urban nihilist poetry and fiction. The outgrowth of a reading series begun in a New York City nightclub in 1993.
**http://mosaic.echonyc.com/~interjackie/verbal/
issue.html**

Verbiage Magazine "Showcasing great short fiction since 1994." Accepts submissions.
http://www.boutell.com/verbiage/

Webster's Weekly Mostly personal essays on various aspects of modern life.
http://www.awa.com/w2/

Word A well-designed and consistently intriguing magazine of arts and culture.
http://www.word.com/

The Words of the Tyrtle A one-person creation of Sage Lunsford, including the essay "Secret Adventures of 8 Feline Cohorts"—"A must-see for anyone who has been held up at claw-point, stomped on at five o'clock in the morning, or scowled at for wet food."
http://www.best.com/~tyrtle/index.html

Writer's Edge A zine aimed at writers: reviews, advice, and resources.
http://www.nashville.net/~edge/the-edge/index.html

Zuzu's Petals Literary Resource One of the best sites on the Web for readers. Home of *Zuzu's Petals Literary Quarterly*, a high-quality Web literary review. Fiction, poetry, essays, and more—submissions encouraged. This site also offers an excellent selection of links to resources elsewhere on the Net, but there is an enormous amount of fascinating material right here. Named, incidentally, for Jimmy Stewart's daughter in *It's a Wonderful Life*.
http://www.hway.net/zuzu/index.htm

USENET NEWSGROUPS
  alt.etext
  alt.zines
  rec.mag.fsfnet

ON-LINE SERVICES

The WELL: Factsheet Five Conference
An electronic extension of the traditional paper magazine of the same name. A comprehensive review of the print zine scene.

Magazines

The following is a selection of Net sites established by print magazines and journals. The amount of the content of the print versions of these magazines that publishers choose to make available free on-line varies considerably. Some offer just a few excerpts to whet the reader's appetite, and usually include a form allowing those interested to subscribe on-line. Other magazines, notably *The Atlantic Monthly* (**http://www2.TheAtlantic.com/Atlantic/**), put almost the entire contents of the print magazine on-line (and, in the case of *The Atlantic*, offer additional features to on-line browsers not found in the print version). The theory behind such apparent largesse seems to be that, since few people will actually read the entire magazine on their computer screens, putting the whole thing on-line is really the most effective way to catch a potential subscriber's attention.

A glimpse into one possible future of magazines on the Net is afforded by *Salon* (**http://www.salon1999.com**), a Web-based magazine devoted to culture and the arts.

Salon covers issues of substance with a depth and style rare in on-line publications. It also has established an on-line conferencing system where readers can discuss articles in the magazine.

The oldest repository of general interest magazines on-line is the

Electronic Newsstand
http://www.enews.com/

which offers excerpts from hundreds of magazines (usually a few articles from the current issue), as well as subscription information. The limitations of the Gopher-based text-only format, however, have led many magazines to establish their own independent presences on the Web. An overview of magazines available on the Net can be found at the following sites:

Electronic Magazines A good international list.
http://www.abc.hu/unix/magazines.html

Starting Point—Magazines A roundup of magazines on-line.
http://www.stpt.com/magazine.html

The following are a few notable examples of magazine Web sites. As usual, if you don't see your favorite here, it doesn't mean it doesn't exist on the Net—just search at Yahoo (**http://www.yahoo.com**) or one of the other search engines listed on page 127 and you may be pleasantly surprised.

Advertising Age
http://www.adage.com/

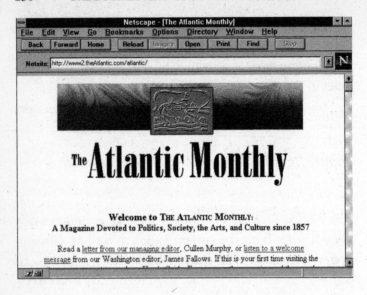

<u>The Atlantic Monthly</u> Most of the print magazine on-line.
http://www2.TheAtlantic.com/Atlantic

<u>The American Prospect</u>
http://epn.org/prospect.html

<u>Barron's</u>
http://www.enews.com/magazines/barrons/

<u>Business Week</u>
http://www.businessweek.com

<u>Condé Nast Traveler Online</u>
http://www.cntraveler.com/

<u>Epicurious</u> An on-line combination of *Bon Appetit* and *Gourmet* magazines.
http://www.epicurious.com/epicurious/home2.html

Hearst Multimedia Online Newsstand *Esquire, Cosmopolitan, Popular Mechanics,* and more on-line.
http://mmnewsstand.com

Life Magazine
http://pathfinder.com/Life

Maclean's Canada's national newsweekly magazine.
gopher://gopher.enews.com/11/collected/macleans/

Mother Jones
http://www.mojones.com

New Republic
http://www.enews.com/magazines/tnr/

ONE An African-American journal of art, music, and politics.
http://www.clark.net/pub/conquest/one/home.html

The Paris Review
http://www.voyagerco.com/PR/

People Magazine
http://pathfinder.com/people/

Premiere Magazine On-line version of the entertainment magazine.
http://www.premieremag.com

Private Eye Net version of the British satirical magazine.
http://www.intervid.co.uk/intervid/eye/gateway.html

Redbook
http://homearts.com/rb/toc/00rbhpc1.htm

Smithsonian Magazine
http://www.si.edu/resource/simag/start.htm

Der Spiegel German news magazine.
http://www.spiegel.de/nda/spiegel/index.html

Sports Illustrated
http://www.pathfinder.com/si/welcome.html

Time Magazine
http://www.pathfinder.com/time/
timehomepage.html

Time Warner Pathfinder Gateway to a variety of Time
Warner magazines.
http://www.pathfinder.com

US News Online From U.S. News and World Report Inc.
http://www2.USNews.com/usnews/main.htm

The UTNE LENS Web site of the *Utne Reader* magazine.
http://www.utne.com/lens/

Washington Free Press
http://www.speakeasy.org/wfpl

Wired Magazine
http://www.hotwired.com/wired/

USENET NEWSGROUP
  rec.mag

ON-LINE SERVICES
In general, the on-line services' versions of popular magazines contain features, such as extensive archives of past articles, not available in the free Web versions of the same
magazines.

America Online: Magazines

The full text of a variety of general-interest magazines on-line, many with searchable archives and discussion forums:

Atlantic Monthly
Consumer Reports
National Geographic Online
Omni Magazine Online
Saturday Review Online
The Smithsonian
The New Republic
Wired Magazine
Worth Magazine
Time Magazine

CompuServe: FORTUNE on CompuServe (GO FORTUNE)

Members can access each new issue, including graphs and photos. They can also search through eight years of back issues.

CompuServe: Magazine Database Plus (GO MAGDB)

Full-text articles from more than 200 publications.

CompuServe: PEOPLE Magazine Daily Edition (GO PEOTDY)

CompuServe: DER SPIEGEL Forum (GO SPIEGEL)

Access full-text articles and interact with the editors of Germany's leading weekly news magazine.

CompuServe: US News Online (GO USNCUR)
Access to the articles and images in the current issue of
U.S. News and World Report.

**CompuServe: U.S. News and World Report Article
Database (GO USNBAK)**
Provides full-text articles. Database contains over 12,000
articles.

Microsoft Network: The New Republic
A weekly journal of political opinion, literature, and art
reviews.

Microsoft Network: The American Spectator
On-line extension of popular opinion magazine. Offers a
chat room, bulletin board, archives, daily news summaries,
editorial comments, and special events with writers and
conservative commentators.

Newspapers and Other News Sources

Browsing the Net will never be a substitute for reading a
good daily newspaper, but there are a growing number of
serious news journals on the Web. Even many small
newspapers have established on-line editions, which can
provide a valuable glimpse into the news from faraway
places that may not make it into your local paper.

INDEXES OF NEWSPAPERS

Editor & Publisher Home Page Offers features on print
media as well as a list of links to on-line newspapers.
http://www.mediainfo.com/edpub/

The European Journalism Page Links to many European publications.
http://www.demon.co.uk/eurojournalism/

Greek Newspapers
http://www.spark.net.gr/perip_e.html

LC Newspaper and Current Periodical Room Newspaper Links A comprehensive index from the U.S. Library of Congress.
http://lcweb.loc.gov/global/ncp/extnewsp.html

NewsLink Features 469 newspaper, 360 broadcast, 508 magazine, and 467 special links, plus surveys and "Top 10" lists.
http://www.newslink.org/menu.html

The Omnivore Excellent news source with links to many unusual publications.
http://way.net/omnivore/

Taxi's Electronic Newspapers A good selection of on-line newspapers.
http://webwise.deltanet.com/users/taxicat/e_papers.html

UNCG's News and Newspapers Online Another good index of newspapers on-line.
http://webwise.uncg.edu/~cecarr/news/

WebWise—Library Print publications and broadcast media with on-line presences.
http://webwise.walcoff.com/library/index.html

NEWSPAPERS

Boston Globe
http://www.boston.com/globe/glohome.htm

The Christian Science Monitor
http://www.csmonitor.com

Daily Record and Sunday Mail From the U.K.
http://www.record-mail.co.uk/rm/drsm/front1.html

The Daily Yomiuri (Japan)
http://www.yomiuri.co.jp/

The Electronic Telegraph An excellent on-line newspaper from the U.K. Free, but requires registration.
http://www.telegraph.co.uk

Evening Times Online (Scotland)
http://web1.cims.co.uk/eveningtimes/

The Gate A joint on-line project of the *San Francisco Chronicle* and the *San Francisco Examiner*.
http://www.sfgate.com

The Guardian WebSite From the U.K.
http://www.guardian.co.uk/

The Haight Ashbury Free Press A vintage alternative newspaper published in San Francisco.
http://www.webcom.com/haight

The Hindu A popular English-language newspaper in India.
http://www.webpage.com/hindu/current/weekly.html

Hong Kong Standard Newspapers
http://www.hkstandard.com

The Irish Times
http://www.irish-times.com

The Jerusalem Post
http://www.jpost.co.il/

Jewish Post of New York Online
http://jewishpost.nais.com/jewishpost/

Mercury Center Home Page *San Jose Mercury* home
page.
http://www.sjmercury.com/

The NandO Times One of the oldest and best of the
on-line newspapers.
http://www2.nando.net/nt/

The New York Times on the Web Free access to most of
each day's issue, including classified ads.
http://www.nytimes.com

The Observer Life Magazine Supplement to the
Observer newspaper in England.
http://www.observer.co.uk/

The St. Petersburg Press (Russia)
http://www.spb.su/sppress/

USA Today
http://web.usatoday.com/news/

Wall Street Journal News, features, and columns.
http://www.wsj.com

The Washington Times National Weekly
http://www.washtimes-weekly.com

OTHER SOURCES OF NEWS

Associated Press Free news briefs, updated frequently.
http://www.trib.com/NEWS/APwire.html

CBS News: UTTMlink "Up-to-the-minute," in case you
were wondering.
http://uttm.com/

CNN Interactive News features from the television news
network.
http://www.cnn.com/

Crayon Crayon lets you design your own daily "newspaper" compiled from free on-line sources—every time
you click on the Crayon bookmark in your Web
browser, you get a new "edition."
http://crayon.net

Digipresse French on-line news agency.
http://www.imaginet.fr/digiweb/

Free Speech Web An on-line newsletter that features ex-
posés of "media abuse."
http://www.GrapevineNews.com/callme

<u>Jinn</u> Pacific News Service's biweekly on-line magazine.
http://www.pacificnews.org/jinn/

<u>Media Online Yellow Pages</u> A directory of media outlets
and contacts.
http://www.webcom.com/~nlnnet/yellowp.html

<u>NewsPage Home Page</u> News retrieval service. Requires
registration and charges a fee for full-text articles.
http://www.newspage.com/

<u>Personal Journal Home Page</u> Customized news, fee-
based service.
http://bis.dowjones.com/pj.html

<u>WWW WorldNews Today</u> A Web-based feature that
gathers news from a wide range of sources.
http://www.fwi.com/wnt/wnt.html

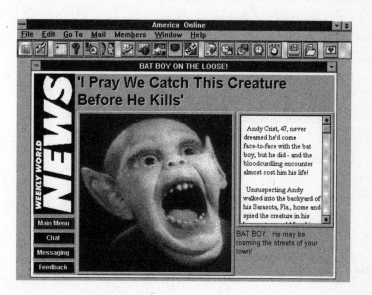

<u>YO! (Youth Outlook)</u> A bimonthly news journal of youth culture.
http://www.pacificnews.org/yo/

USENET NEWSGROUPS
 alt.journalism
 alt.journalism.newspapers

ON-LINE SERVICES

America Online: Chicago Tribune
Full text and searchable archives.

America Online: San Jose Mercury News
Full text and searchable archives.

America Online: New York Times
Full text and searchable archives.

America Online: Weekly World News
Full text and archives. Features Elvis sightings, the Bat Boy, and other stories mysteriously not covered by the mainstream media.

CompuServe: Detroit Free Press (GO DFM)

CompuServe: Neue Zuercher Zeitung (GO ZUERCHER)
The *Neue Zuercher Zeitung* newspaper offers news, analysis, and background information about economic and political events from around the world. In German.

CompuServe: Newspaper Archives (GO NEWSARCHIVE)

Full-text articles from over 61 U.S., Canadian, and U.K. newspapers. Members can search in the archives by entering keywords appearing in headlines or article text, a topic of interest, or a specific date range. Most of the databases range from the late 1980s to the present.

CompuServe: News Source USA

A comprehensive collection of major U.S. magazines, newspapers, and special features.

CompuServe: Sueddeutsche Zeitung (GO SUEDDEUT)

The *Sueddeutsche Zeitung*, a leading German newspaper.

CompuServe: UK Newspaper Library (GO UKPAPERS)

The U.K. Newspaper Library contains articles from the leading British papers, including *The Daily Telegraph* and *Sunday Telegraph*, *The European*, *The Financial Times*, *The Guardian*, *The Times* and *Sunday Times*, *The Independent*, and *The Independent on Sundays* and *Today*.

Microsoft Network: USA Today

Full text of the newspaper once characterized as "television you can wrap fish in."

Prodigy: Prodigy Newsstand

Access to numerous magazines (*American Heritage*, *Condé Nast Traveler*, *Consumer Reports*, *Newsweek Interactive*,

Atlantic Monthly, Life, George, The Utne Reader, The Village Voice, Washingtonian, Smithsonian, etc.), plus newspapers such as the *Houston Chronicle*. Complete *Newsday* archives available.

LIBRARIES AND REFERENCE SOURCES

Dictionaries and Other Language Resources

Inasmuch as the Internet sprang from academia and remains largely a written medium, the vast range of language resources available on-line is not surprising. On-line dictionaries and glossaries abound, and the Internet community's love of words and language is evidenced by the wide variety of language resources on-line.

DICTIONARIES

The ARTFL French-English Dictionary
**http://humanities.uchicago.edu/forms_unrest/
FR-ENG.html**

English-Slovene/Slovene-English Dictionary
http://www.fer.uni-lj.si/dictionary/a2s.html

Hypertext Webster Interface A free on-line English dictionary.
http://c.gp.cs.cmu.edu:5103/prog/webster

Japanese-English Dictionary
http://enterprise.ic.gc.ca/cgi-bin/j-e/

On-line Dictionaries and Glossaries A good directory of what's available on-line.
http://www.rahul.net/lai/glossaries.html

Online English-Russian Bilingual Dictionary
http://www.elvis.ru/cgi-bin/mtrans

Pedro's Dictionaries Links to an amazing assortment of multilingual and special dictionaries.
http://www.public.iastate.edu/~pedro/dictionaries.html

OTHER GENERAL LANGUAGE RESOURCES

Addicted to Words An examination of words in all their social roles.
http://www.morestuff.com/words/a2wortop.htm

Archive of Endangered, Special, or Fun Words
http://www.infi.net/~rvance/esofword.html

British Slang Glossary
http://eno.princeton.edu/~ben/vocab/vocab.html

The Cool Word of the Day Page
http://www.dsu.edu/projects/word_of_day/word.html

The Cymdeithas Madog Home Page Learn Welsh on the Web.
http://tpowel.comdis.lsumc.edu/cymraeg/madog.htm

An Elementary Grammar Help at last for the gerund-challenged.
http://www.hiway.co.uk/~ei/intro.html

The English Server at CMU An extensive and well-designed site with links to hundreds of language resources.
http://english.hss.cmu.edu/

Filipino Slang
http://www.pitt.edu/~filipina/slang.html

French Slang You, you, son of a poodle, you!
http://www.easynet.co.uk/home/fslang.htm

Grammar Hotline Directory Is the question of "which or that" the one that (which?) is driving you around the bend? Here's a list of experts you can call, arranged by state.
http://www.infi.net/tcc/hotline.html

Grammar and Style Notes Jack Lynch sets you straight.
http://www.english.upenn.edu/~jlynch/grammar.html

The Human-Languages Page An outstanding collection of linguistic resources, arranged by language.
http://www.willamette.edu/~tjones/LanguagePage.html

Keith Ivey's English Usage Page Helpful hints on grammar.
http://www.webcom.com/~kcivey/engusage/

The Jargon File—Greek Dictionary of Computing Terminology
http://www.cnam.fr/Jargon/

Klingon Language Institute Phasers on stun—they're serious.
http://kli.org/

<u>Lingo Rules</u> Current slang and lingo.
http://indy6.cpedu.rug.nl:8084/lingo.rules.html

<u>The Modern Language Centre</u> A vast collection of language resources.
http://www.oise.on.ca/webstuff/departments/mlc1.html

<u>OED News</u> News from the folks who bring you the Oxford English Dictionary.
http://www.oup.co.uk/newoed.html

<u>Propaganda Analysis Home Page</u> You are what you read.
http://carmen.artsci.washington.edu/propaganda/home.htm

<u>StreetSpeak</u> What young people are speaking, supposedly.
http://www.jayi.com/Fishnet/StreetSpeak/

<u>Twists, Slugs, and Roscoes: A Glossary of Hardboiled Slang</u> A glossary compiled from a variety of detective novels.
http://www.io.org/~buff/slang.html

<u>Vietnam Veteran's Terminology and Slang</u>
http://grunt.space.swri.edu/glossary.htm

<u>The Weekly Idiom</u> Each week, an explanation of a new English idiom and an accompanying sample dialogue.
http://www.comenius.com/idiom/index.html

<u>Word for Word</u> A dandy language column from Down Under.
http://peg.pegasus.oz.au/~toconnor/

The Word Detective A language column written by yours truly.
http://www.users.interport.net/~words1/

Word Play A good collection of links to Net sites devoted to having fun with words.
http://homepage.interaccess.com/~wolinsky/word.htm

Wordwatch A fascinating weekly commentary on current English.
http://titania.cobuild.collins.co.uk:80/wordwatch.html

The World-Wide Web Virtual Library: Linguistics A comprehensive collection of resource links.
http://www.brown.edu/Departments/Cog-Ling-Sci/ lingdir/dictionary.html

USENET NEWSGROUPS
    alt.usage.english
    bit.listserv.words-1
    misc.education.language.english
    sci.lang

ON-LINE SERVICES

America Online: Merriam-Webster
A good collection of useful M-W offerings, including the Merriam-Webster Bookstore, Collegiate Dictionary, Kids' Dictionary, Medical Dictionary, Thesaurus, World Histories, and Word of the Day. Word Histories Forum features interesting discussions of word origins.

The WELL: Language Conference
Discussion of all aspects of language and its role in society.

The WELL: The Words Conference
A place to discuss the vagaries, peculiarities, oddities, beauties, and inanities of language.

Libraries

Contrary to popular impression (unfortunately), it is rarely possible to access the contents of books held by libraries via the Internet. You can, however, browse the catalogs of most libraries, and many have extensive research materials available on-line. Many libraries also make available on-line exhibits of archival material and historical documents, such as the remarkable *American Memory* (**http://rs6.loc.gov:80/amhome.html**) exhibit mounted by the U.S. Library of Congress. In addition many library sites maintain extensive lists of links to other sites of interest on the Internet.

Although libraries are in the process of converting their catalogs to make them fully accessible via the Web, the process is slow. In many cases, catalogs currently are available only via a telnet connection (see Chapter 3 for an explanation of how telnet works). It is common for these libraries to maintain a Web page offering general information about the library and a hypertext link, which will then initiate a telnet session with the actual library catalog. Fortunately, you'll almost always find information about how to log into (and log out from) the library's telnet system right there on the Web page, and with just a little practice you'll have access to the catalogs of some of the largest libraries in the world. Don't be afraid to experiment—you can't break anything.

General information about libraries on the Net and directories of libraries on-line around the world can be found at:

<u>American Library Association</u> Founded in 1876, the ALA is the oldest and largest library association in the world.
http://www.ala.org/

<u>Bookwire Directory of Libraries</u> More than 500 libraries on-line worldwide, indexed by location and name.
http://www.bookwire.com/index/libraries.html

<u>Library Catalogs With Web Interfaces</u>
http://www.lib.ncsu.edu/staff/morgan/alcuin/ wwwedcatalogs.html

<u>Library WWW Servers</u> A worldwide directory of libraries on the Web.
http://sunsite.berkeley.edu/libweb/

<u>Literature Webliography</u> A guide to scholarly library resources.
http://www.lib.lsu.edu/hum/lit.html

<u>Virtual Libraries on the Web</u>
http://www.w3.org/hypertext/DataSources/ bySubject/Virtual_libraries/Overview.html

<u>Where the Wild Things are—A Librarians' Guide to the Net</u>
http://web.sau.edu/cwis/Internet/wild/index.htm

Specific libraries (or subject-oriented directories of libraries) worth a visit include:

Association of Research Libraries
http://arl.cni.org/

Australian Libraries
http://info.anu.edu.au/ozlib/ozlib.html

Chicago Public Library
http://cpl.lib.uic.edu/

Gabriel The information server for Europe's National Libraries.
http://portico.bl.uk/gabriel/en/welcome.html

INFOMINE-UC Riverside Libraries
http://lib-www.ucr.edu/

Library of Congress
http://lcweb.loc.gov/homepage/lchp.html

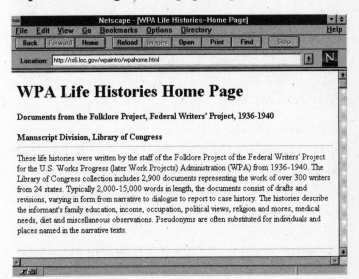

Netscape - [WPA Life Histories–Home Page]

File Edit View Go Bookmarks Options Directory · · · Help

Back | Forward | Home | Reload | Images | Open | Print | Find | Stop

Location: http://rs6.loc.gov/wpaintro/wpahome.html

WPA Life Histories Home Page

Documents from the Folklore Project, Federal Writers' Project, 1936-1940

Manuscript Division, Library of Congress

These life histories were written by the staff of the Folklore Project of the Federal Writers' Project for the U.S. Works Progress (later Work Projects) Administration (WPA) from 1936-1940. The Library of Congress collection includes 2,900 documents representing the work of over 300 writers from 24 states. Typically 2,000-15,000 words in length, the documents consist of drafts and revisions, varying in form from narrative to dialogue to report to case history. The histories describe the informant's family education, income, occupation, political views, religion and mores, medical needs, diet and miscellaneous observations. Pseudonyms are often substituted for individuals and places named in the narrative texts.

National Library of Canada
http://www.nlc-bnc.ca/ehome.htm

National Library of New Zealand
http://www.natlib.govt.nz/

National Network of Libraries of Medicine
http://www.nnlm.nlm.nih.gov/

New York Public Library Home Page
http://www.nypl.org/

Portico—The British Library
http://portico.bl.uk/

Stanford University Digital Libraries Project
http://www-diglib.stanford.edu/diglib/

The Virginia Library and Information Network
http://www.vsla.edu/

USENET NEWSGROUP
   soc.libraries.talk

Reference Sources

The good news is that there are many useful reference sources available on the Net for free. The bad news is that most current editions of dictionaries and encyclopedias are covered by copyright and are not available to the public on the Internet, except for *Encyclopedia Britannica*, available by paid subscription (see below). Some other sources are on-line but simply not accessible to the public—the *Oxford English Dictionary*, for example, is currently available on-line only to students at universities that have paid licensing fees to Oxford University Press.

Each of the commercial on-line services offers its sub-scribers access to a selection of current reference works, as well as more sophisticated databases. If you're planning to conduct serious research on-line, it may be worth sub-scribing to one of these services.

Many of the reference works that are available for free on the Net are older editions of popular works (*Bartlett's Quotations*, *Roget's Thesaurus*, etc.) now not covered by copyright and, consequently, in the public domain.

There are several directories of on-line reference works available on the Net. Among them:

The Information SuperLibrary A good index of refer-ence sources on-line.
http://www.mcp.com/

On-line Reference Works Another good roundup of ref-erence resources.
http://www.cs.cmu.edu/Web/references.html

The Virtual Reference Desk An excellent overview of on-line reference sources.
http://thorplus.lib.purdue.edu/reference/index.html

INFORMATION ABOUT THE U.S. GOVERNMENT
The U.S. Federal government has made a variety of use-ful information available on-line. Other information is available from nongovernmental Net sites, such as law schools. A few notable sources:

Copyright Clearance Center Online
http://www.openmarket.com/copyright/

Department of the Treasury: IRS Tax forms, assistance, and information. They'll even come to your house if you ask nicely.
http://www.irs.ustreas.gov/

Federal Bureau of Investigation
http://www.fbi.gov

U.S. Copyright Office Home Page
http://lcweb.loc.gov/copyright/

U.S. Department of Health
http://www.os.dhhs.gov/

U.S. Patent and Trademark Office
http://www.uspto.gov/

U.S. Tax Code On-Line
http://www.fourmilab.ch/ustax/ustax.html

U.S. Trademark Law
http://www.law.cornell.edu/topics/trademark.html

The White House Sign the guest book and read the First Cat's biography.
http://www.whitehouse.gov/

OTHER HELPFUL REFERENCE RESOURCES

AT&T Internet Toll Free 800 Directory
http://www.tollfree.att.net/dir800/

Bartlett's Familiar Quotations 1901 edition.
http://www.columbia.edu/acis/bartleby/bartlett/

CLIO—The National Archives Information Server
Home of the National Archives and Records Administration. Offers on-line searches of the Federal Register,
the John F. Kennedy Assassination Records Collection,
and other databases.
http://www.nara.gov/

Encyclopedia Britannica Online Subscription-based:
$150/year, plus $25 setup fee.
http://www.eb.com/

The Intelligence Community Information about the
folks who gather information about you.
http://www.odci.gov/ic/

The Internet Movie Database Everything you ever
wanted to know about movies—casts, directors, etc.
http://us.imdb.com

NOAA Central Library (National Oceanic and
Atmospheric Administration) A collection of more
than one million books, journals, technical reports,
microfiche, microfilm, compact disks, and databases.
http://www.lib.noaa.gov/

REFLAW A reference source for law-related issues from
the Washburn University School of Law Library in
Topeka, Kansas.
http://lawlib.wuacc.edu/washlaw/reflaw/reflaw.html

ON-LINE SERVICES

America Online: Compton's Encyclopedia
More than 35,000 articles searchable by subject or keyword.

America Online: General Reference
A variety of searchable reference works, including *National Geographic Atlas*, *The Dictionary of Cultural Literacy*, *Merriam-Webster's Collegiate Dictionary*, *Merriam-Webster's Medical Dictionary*, *The Columbia Concise Encyclopedia*, *The Macmillan Information SuperLibrary*, *Merriam-Webster's Thesaurus*, and *Merriam-Webster's Word Histories*.

CompuServe: Comprehensive Core Medical Library AIDS Articles (GO CCMLAIDS)
People interested in AIDS research can use this searchable medical library to find full-text AIDS-related articles. Sources include medical reference books, textbooks, and medical journals, such as the *New England Journal of Medicine, Science, and Nature*.

CompuServe: Grolier's Encyclopedia (GO ENCYCLOPEDIA)
The on-line edition of *Grolier's Academic American Encyclopedia*—over 30,000 articles and 10 million words, updated and revised four times a year.

CompuServe: Government Publications (GO GPO)
A catalog of government publications, books, and subscription services. Any CompuServe member with a valid MasterCard or Visa can order on-line any publication from the U.S. Government Printing Office.

CompuServe: Information Please General Almanac (GO GENALMANAC)
Contains subjects ranging from astronomy to the environment, from nutrition to world statistics.

CompuServe: IQuest (GO IQUEST)

IQuest, CompuServe's on-line information retrieval service, offers access to over 400 databases. Source materials include magazines, newspapers, indexes, conference proceedings, directories, books, newsletters, government documents, dissertations, encyclopedias, patent records, and reference guides.

CompuServe: IQuest Medical InfoCenter (GO IQMEDICINE)

An on-line reference tool for finding information on medical practice, research, pharmaceutical news, and allied health studies. InfoCenter databases provide access to information extracted from published sources such as journals, books, and government publications about health and medicine.

CompuServe: Legal Research Center (GO LEGALRC)

Access to seven databases containing articles from more than 750 law journals.

CompuServe: PaperChase (GO PAPERCHASE)

Access to MEDLINE, the National Library of Medicine's database of references to biomedical literature. Included are over 7 million references from 4,000 journals dating from January 1966 to the present.

Microsoft Network: Microsoft Encarta Encyclopedia

Encarta Forum contains the North American edition of the Encarta Encyclopedia.

Microsoft Network: The Princeton Review
The Princeton Review is the source for expert information related to college, graduate, and professional school.

Prodigy: Compton's Encyclopedia
Offers more than 35,000 articles, searchable by subject or keyword. New multimedia features include built-in sound and music files.

Prodigy: Homework Helper
Not just for kids—a remarkably sophisticated information search and retrieval program. Database includes more than 1,500 books, 100 newspapers, and a wide variety of technical journals.

WRITING RESOURCES

Something about the Internet attracts writers (it must be all those words . . .), making it a great place to find advice on writing, as well as writers' resources by the bushel. Thanks to the Net, you can even take advantage of high-powered creative writing programs at major universities through the OWLs (on-line writing laboratories) listed below. The best thing about the Net for a writer, of course, is that it's chock-full of people eager to read what you've written—many of the sites listed below welcome submissions.

General Writing Resources

Essays for Writers Inspiration and guidance from other writers.
http://www.interlog.com/~ohi/inkspot/essays.html

More Writers' Links An excellent list of links to all sorts of writing resources on the Net.
http://www.interlog.com/~ohi/inkspot/links.html

Online Resource for Writers A directory of Internet resources.
http://www.ume.maine.edu/~wcenter/resource.html

Reader's & Writer's Resource Page A comprehensive page devoted to making life easier for writers. Many valuable links to resources elsewhere on the Net.
http://www.diane.com/readers/

Write On-Line A directory of on-line writing groups, including those available on the commercial on-line services.
http://www.writepage.com/riteline.htm

The Write Place Tools, inspiration, and resources for all kinds of writing. Opportunities for you to contribute your own writing to the page.
http://www.rio.com/~wplace/

Writers Groups A listing of writing groups that meet in person.
http://www.writepage.com/groups.htm

Writers on the Net Offers a collection of services for writers and aspiring writers, including on-line classes and tutoring via e-mail.
http://www.writers.com

University Writing Programs and Writing Laboratories

On-line writing labs are wonderful sources of information of use to writers—grammar guides, style manuals, resource lists, and specialized guidance on everything from how to write a research paper to the proper format for a doctoral dissertation. These pages also offer lists of links to other writing resources on the Internet.

Dakota State University Online Writing Lab (OWL)
http://www.dsu.edu:80/departments/liberal/cola/OWL/

Purdue On-Line Writing Lab (OWL)
http://owl.english.purdue.edu/

The Rensselaer Writing Center Handouts
http://www.rpi.edu/dept/llc/writecenter/web/handouts.html

Texas Undergraduate Writing Center
http://www.utexas.edu/depts/uwc/.html/handout.html

University of Michigan Online Writing Lab
http://www.umich.edu/~nesta/OWL/owl.html

Writing (University of Michigan)
http://www.lib.umich.edu/chouse/inter/165.html

Writing at MU (Missouri University)
http://www.missouri.edu/~wleric/writery.htm.

Journalism Resources

American Journalism Review A comprehensive guide to journalism resources on the World Wide Web; includes

information on awards and fellowships available to journalists.
http://www.inform.umd.edu:8080/News/AJR/ ajr.html

<u>Columbia Journalism Review</u> Web site of the premier American journalism review. Features a collection of the articles and photos that won Pulitzers.
http://www.cjr.org/

<u>Internet Newsroom</u> "Your Guide to Electronic Fact-gathering"—how to use the resources on the Net to do research.
http://www.dgsys.com/~editors/index.html

<u>Media Watchdog</u> A collection of on-line media-watch resources, including specific media criticism articles and information about media-watch groups.
http://theory.lcs.mit.edu/~mernst/media/

<u>Newspapers That Take E-mail Submissions (via Gopher)</u>
gopher://gopher.std.com:70/00/periodicals/ Middlesex-News/medialist

<u>Pulitzer Prizes</u> A complete list of winners, by year.
http://www.pulitzer.org/

<u>The Reporter's Internet Survival Guide</u> An AP reporter's Internet resource list.
http://www.qns.com/~casey/

<u>Reporters' Resource Page</u> Another good directory of information sources on the Net.
http://www.uttm.com/reporter/

Helpful Resources for Writers

Fiction Therapy Group A collaborative writing project that seeks to help writers express themselves. Visitors can contribute to ongoing stories and poems. Worth a look, but the experiment seems to have gotten a bit out of control.
http://asylum.cid.com/fiction/fiction.html

Grammar and Style Guides for Writers The rules of the road to success.
http://www.interlog.com/~ohi/inkspot/style.html

Grammar and Style Notes More handy tips on style questions.
http://www.english.upenn.edu/~jlynch/grammar.html

HTML Basics and Links World Wide Web design resources.
http://info.med.yale.edu/caim/M_Resources.HTML

Internet Directory of Literary Agents
http://www.bocklabs.wisc.edu/ims/agents.html

Internet Fiction Writer's Club Submit your stories (any genre), and a panel of reviewers will give you their honest opinions and constructive advice. The best stories submitted will be published in an anthology. Complete details on the Web page.
http://haven.uniserve.com/~tsauder/

Quotes for Writers Jazz up your writing with bits of someone else's.
http://www.interlog.com/~ohi/inkspot/quotes.html

Resources for Writers and Writing Instructors A good roundup of on-line resources.
http://www.english.upenn.edu:80/~jlynch/writing.html

Resources for Writers on the Web Another directory for writers.
http://bel.avonibp.co.uk/bricolage/resources/ websites/ahart.html

Thinking and Writing Clearly Tips on clearing the fuzz from your noggin.
http://www.midnightbeach.com/hs/clarity.htm

Writers' Organizations

American Society of Journalists and Authors
http://www.eskimo.com/~brucem/asja.htm

National Writers Union Home Page
http://www.nwu.org/nwu/

Screenwriting

Internet Screenwriter's Network
http://www.screenwriters.com/screennet.html

Screenwriters Online Resources, discussions, and a chance to interact with successful screenwriters on-line.
http://www.leonardo.net/insider

Children's Writing Resources

Children's Book Council On-line site of a trade association of children's publishers.
http://www.cbcbooks.org/

<u>Children's Writing Resource Center</u> A directory of on-line resources.
http://www.mindspring.com/~cbi

<u>Inkspot</u> An excellent compilation of resources for children's writers.
http://www.interlog.com/~ohi/inkspot/ home.html

Diaries and Collective Writing Projects

<u>Bad Writing Project</u> Nothing raises the spirits like a little *schadenfreude.* No matter how bad a writer you may think you are, you'll never be this bad. Contributions welcomed.
http://nyx10.cs.du.edu:8001/~rebell/writprj.html

<u>Notes and Journals</u> Read the journals of three friends recounting a shared reality.
http://www.rrnet.com/~nakamura/picbooks/ index.html

<u>The Passing Show</u> A do-it-yourself commentary on life. Visitors may add what they like.
http://www.europa.com/~kbsadler/passingshow.html

USENET NEWSGROUPS
   alt.prose   Original writings, fiction and otherwise.
   alt.prose.d   Discussion of alt.prose articles.
   misc.writing   Discussion of writing in all of its forms.
   misc.writing.screenplays   Aspects of writing and
      selling screenplays.

ON-LINE SERVICES

America Online: Writers' Club
Includes Message Center, Writers' Club Libraries, The Writers' Club Conference, and The Writers' Workshop.

CompuServe: Literary Forum (GO LITFORUM)
A gathering place for professional writers, literature readers, journalists, humorists, and those with an interest in any related field. Included are sections on poetry, controversial topics, fiction, science fiction, comics, humor, and journalism.

CompuServe: Writer's Forum (GO WRITER)
Numerous workshops, including poetry, novels, and short pieces.

Microsoft Network: Screenwriters Studios
Discussion of the craft of screenwriting, for both veterans and novices.

Microsoft Network: Writing Forum
A forum for professional and aspiring writers of all ages, in all genres.

Prodigy: Writing Workshop
An excellent Web-based resource for writers. Members discuss each other's stories and submissions. The Fiction Therapy Group and the Script Emporium include stories to read or to finish. Moderator Carol Hayes, newspaper and magazine writer, also leads workshops off-line.

The WELL: Byline—Freelance Writers Conference

For freelance nonfiction writers who want to swap advice on marketing themselves and their work, share information on practical business issues like health insurance and home offices, and exchange tips on research and writing.

The WELL: Media Conference

Discussion of all aspects of print and electronic journalism, with special emphasis on the legal and ethical problems facing practitioners.

The WELL: Periodical/Newsletter Conference

Publishers of newsletters and other small periodicals share resources and information.

The WELL: The Writers Conference

The large number of professional writers on The WELL make this conference a good place to find answers to questions regarding submissions, query letters, grants and awards, writers' colonies, writer's block, and the latest news from the world of publishing.

SOURCES OF INFORMATION ABOUT THE INTERNET

The best place to find news and information about the Internet is, not surprisingly, on the Internet. In fact, the Net never seems to tire of talking about itself. Below are some helpful sites.

<u>Aether Madness</u> The full text of a print book about the Net. Lots of information in plain English.
http://www.neo.com/Aether/

<u>c/net on-line</u> Home page of a TV show about the Net; very good features.
http://www.cnet.com/

<u>Cyberspace Today</u> News about the Net.
http://www.cybertoday.com/cybertoday/

<u>CyberWire Dispatches</u> Home page for an excellent newsletter about the Net.
http://cyberwerks.com:70/cyberwire/cwd

<u>EFFweb</u> Home page of the Electronic Frontier Foundation, an organization promoting and defending free speech on the Internet.
http://www.eff.org/

<u>Internet World Homepage</u> Home page of the best U.S. Internet magazine. Perceptive articles and reviews of new Net sites.
http://www.mecklerweb.com/

<u>Jumbo!</u> The best shareware software archive on the Net, for all types of computers.
http://www.jumbo.com/

<u>THE LIST</u> An excellent directory of Internet service providers, arranged by area code.
http://thelist.com/

<u>NetGuide Home Page</u> The self-described TV Guide of the Net.
http://techweb.comp.com/techweb/ng/current

Netree Fascinating page with news from around the Net.
http://www.netree.com

Point Communications Corporation They pick the "Top 5% Web Sites," an award that is taken very seriously, at least by the chosen sites.
http://www.pointcom.com/

Gleason Sackman's Net-Happenings Home page for the indispensable guide to what's new on the Net.
http://www.mid.net:80/NET/

Special Interest Connections The classic Net guide from Scott Yanoff, updated regularly.
http://www.uwm.edu/Mirror/inet.services.html

What's New With NCSA Mosaic From the National Center for Supercomputing Applications, the folks who invented the Mosaic Web browser.
http://www.ncsa.uiuc.edu/SDG/Software/Mosaic/ Docs/whats-new.html

With Morning Coffee A wake-up page with news, humor, and even a daily cartoon.
http://www.interlog.com/~ohi/inkspot/ coffee.html

USENET NEWSGROUPS
  alt.culture.internet
  comp.internet.net-happenings
  news.answers
  rec.answers

Chapter 8

KEEPING UP WITH THE NET: HOW TO STAY ABREAST OF NEW RESOURCES ON THE INTERNET

The newcomer to the Internet often feels like a visitor to a strange new country. There's a new language to be learned, new customs to get used to, and, of course, there's the process of finding your way around. Unfortunately, there's no reliable map of the Internet that you can buy, and even if there were such a map, it would have to be updated nearly every day, for the Internet is growing and changing constantly. Dozens of new sites are launched every day, old favorites change their location or disappear entirely, new Usenet newsgroups are formed, mailing lists are announced, even the software available to roam the Net is being constantly updated.

Fortunately, there are several ways to keep up with developments on the Net. They include mailing lists, Usenet newsgroups, Web pages, e-mail newsletters, and even (gasp!) old-fashioned print-on-paper magazines and books. No single source lists absolutely everything that's new or different on the Net, so most users end up checking several of them every so often. Put together, though, any two or three of these sources will do a pretty good job of keeping you up to date with what's new.

ON-LINE NEWSLETTERS

The Net-Happenings Digest: The easiest way to keep up with the changing landscape of the Net is by subscribing to this e-mail announcement newsletter. It's an especially good way to get news of the Net because it lists new resources of almost all types—Web pages, mailing lists, Net software, other newsletters, and more. *Net Happenings* is available in several forms: as a digest in newsletter format, as a mailing list of individual announcements, or mirrored as a Usenet newsgroup, **comp.internet.net-happenings**. I recommend that you subscribe to the digest form, because a subscription to the mailing list will fill your in box with dozens of messages every day, and postings to the Usenet newsgroup expire fairly quickly on most news servers so you might easily miss an announcement of interest. The digest form also comes with a handy table of contents in each issue, so you can see right away whether there's anything of interest to you.

To subscribe to *The Net-Happenings Digest*, send an e-mail message to **listserv@lists.internic.net**, leaving the subject line blank and the body of the message reading *subscribe Net-happenings-digest your full name*. You can also search the *Net-Happenings* archives, as well as see the most recent issue, at **http://www.mid.net:80/Net/**. If you have something to announce, check out the handy submittal form.

Special Internet Connections: Another good news-letter, which can be had by sending an e-mail message to **listserv@csd.uwm.edu**, subject line blank, message reading *subscribe inetlist your full name*.

The IWatch Digest: Subscribe by sending an e-mail message to **listserv@garcia.com**, with a blank subject line and *subscribe IWatch your full name* in the body.

Seidman's Online Insider: If you're interested in general news about the Net, including technological innovations, censorship, and the evolution of the Net itself, you should subscribe to this newsletter. Send an e-mail message to **listserv@peach.ease.lsoft.com** and in the body of the message type *subscribe on-line-1 your full name*. The *Online Insider* can also be found at **http://www.clark.Net:80/pub/robert/home.html**.

Edupage: Describes itself as "a summary of news items on information technology," but it's much more interesting than it sounds. Send requests to **listproc@educom.unc.edu** and in the body of the message type *subscribe edupage your full name*. The same folks also produce *The Educom Review*, a "bimonthly print magazine on learning, communications, and information technology," so they pay special attention to learning resources on the Net.

USENET NEWSGROUPS

comp.infosystems.www.announce: The place to find announcements of new resources on the Web, so you'll probably want to set your newsreader to subscribe to this group.

rec.arts.books: Many new sites and resources on the Net are announced in this newsgroup.

news.announce.newgroups: For news about new Usenet newsgroups. Most newsreaders, by the way, have a "get new group" feature of some sort, so it's fairly easy to see what new newsgroups your provider has chosen to carry. There's still a strong case to be made for reading news.announce.newgroups, however: if there's a new group that you're interested in reading but your provider has chosen not to pick it up, chances are good that they'll carry it if you ask them nicely.

comp.internet.net-happenings: The *Net Happenings* newsletter (see above) is reposted to this newsgroup.

THE WEB

The Yahoo home page (http://www.yahoo.com): Another good way to keep up with what's new on the Web is to check here every so often, where you'll find what the Yahoo-sters consider notable new sites on the Web.

There are also a growing number of sites that feature

the "Cool Site of the Day" or the like. If you're primarily looking for resources connected to books and reading, however, these sites tend to be a waste of time. The Web pages they pick may be "cool" (especially to those who routinely use the word "cool" in conversation, I suppose), but are rarely intellectually rewarding.

One overlooked way to find new things on the Net is simply to use the search engines of the Web (see Chapter 3 for a listing). Check under such general categories as "Books" or "Libraries." Most of the results you'll get back will already be familiar to you, but there will almost always be a few new jewels in the mix.

MAGAZINES

Magazines (the print-on-paper kind) devoted to the Internet have multiplied rapidly, as have the number of mainstream computer magazines now offering some coverage of the Internet. In general, those magazines aimed specifically at Internet users are far more likely to point you in the right direction than are the general computer magazines, which have proven to be remarkably clueless when it comes to the Net. A few notable Internet-specific magazines worth checking out:

Internet World: Of the Net-specific magazines available, probably the best across the board, combining excellent coverage of the Net itself with frequent features detailing on-line resources in specific areas of interest.

Net Guide, Virtual City, and *The Net* can all be rewarding on occasion, though you'd be well advised to browse their contents pages before investing in any particular issue. One strong point of these three magazines is that they all cover offerings from the major on-line services, so if you access the Net through CompuServe, America Online, or a similar service, you may find helpful pointers to resources there.

Wired can be a good source of news about the Net, but it espouses a heady mix of cyberevangelism and consumerism that some people find annoying. The few specific Internet resources listed in *Wired* almost always fall into the "Cool Site of the Day" category.

.net (that's "dot net"), one of the best magazines devoted to the Internet, is difficult to find in the United States, but is definitely worth the effort. Published in England, *.net* combines excellent coverage of the Internet with a highly literate sense of humor. The one reliable source for *.net* I have found is the Barnes & Noble chain.

BOOKS

Because the Internet is growing so rapidly, the various Internet directories that you will find in bookstores are almost certainly at least slightly outdated by the time they're published, although the best of them will still contain a great deal of valuable information. One Net directory in particular stands out, however:

The Internet Yellow Pages: Of the several directories calling themselves "Internet Yellow Pages" to be found in bookstores, by far the best is this one, by Harley Hahn, published by Osborne McGraw-Hill. Hahn lists resources of all types (Web, Gopher, Usenet, etc.) by subject in a clear and logical format, interspersed with unexpected but welcome bits of humor. This book contains so many neat things that you'll want to log onto the Net immediately after browsing through just a few pages.

Ultimately, your best source of information about new things on the Net is likely to be the Net itself. Remember that simply because you've visited a site once doesn't mean that you've seen it all, and the best sites periodically update themselves with new material and links to other places on the Net.

INDEX

About the Author

Evan Morris's column on words and language, *Words, Wit and Wisdom*, appears in newspapers in the United States, Mexico, and Japan (and is available on the World Wide Web at **http://www.interport.net/~words1**). He also produces the bimonthly newsletter "The Word Detective." Mr. Morris has years of experience on both the Internet and on-line services and the phone bills to prove it. He is married, has one son, and lives in New York City.